Ashes '97
Two Views from
the Boundary

Ashes '97
Two Views from the Boundary

Norman Geras
Ian Holliday

baseline
BOOKS

First published 1997 by
Baseline Book Company
PO Box 8
Tisbury
Wiltshire SP3 6TG

© 1997 Norman Geras and Ian Holliday

All rights reserved. No part of this publication
may be reproduced, stored in a retrieval system,
or transmitted, in any form, or by any means,
electronic, mechanical, photocopying, recording
or otherwise, without prior written permission
from the publisher.

British Library Cataloguing in Publication Data

ISBN 1 897626 11 8

Cover design by Price Watkins
All photographs by Tom Jenkins
Printed and bound by Nuffield Press, Abingdon

Contents

1　Preface

3　First Test, Edgbaston

23　Second Test, Lord's

47　Third Test, Old Trafford

79　Fourth Test, Headingley

107　Fifth Test, Trent Bridge

135　Sixth Test, The Oval

161　Series averages

Preface

We offer, here, a rather different kind of cricket book. Neither of us is a professional writer on the game. We are two spectators, both lovers of cricket as well as keen followers of the England-Australia contest from opposite sides. What we give in these pages is, not only an account of the Tests of 1997 from that dual perspective, but also something of our own participation, on the sidelines, as friends and rivals.

The idea of following this series, attending every day of every match, was hatched between us a while ago. We must have agreed some time in 1996 that 1997 was as good a year as any for turning our dream of following one summer's Ashes battle into reality. The idea of writing a book about it, on the other hand, emerged more haphazardly. In the air between us almost from the start was the thought of keeping diaries of the experience, but right up to the countdown to the first Test, that was about it. Only at Edgbaston on the first morning of the series did we decide to give the project a go by trying to write up our impressions of the day in a form that might be of interest to others. Even then we both spent the evening of that first day wondering whether we would actually have enough to say.

This issue was quickly settled. We did have something to say and found ourselves enjoying saying it. The decision to publish was not taken at once but after friends and family to whom we showed our match reports had encouraged us by their responses. We are very grateful to them, and we take this opportunity of thanking them all for the time they spent reading and commenting on our stuff. They are Erwin (Piwi) Eva, Adèle Geras, Kathryn Holliday and Morris Szeftel. Also, in a separate but no less important category here is Martin Johnson, whose cricket writing both of us have long admired and enjoyed, and who was good enough to give us a friendly and supporting outside view. Paul Cammack, finally, helped us out of a minor fix by suggesting our subtitle. We alone, of course, are responsible for the decision to go public and for what is in the book.

Our accounts were composed in a regular and methodical fashion. At all of the six Tests both of us wrote our reports on each day's play before the next one began; either the same evening or early the following morning. We did not confer. Each of us then subjected his report to stylistic revision at the end of the Test, but permitted himself to make no changes of substance with the benefit of hindsight.

We only exchanged our accounts when both of them had been finalised, the exchange taking place in the period between Tests. The comments of each of us prompted small emendations within the other's account to remove infelicities of one kind and another. In general, however, few changes were made and our accounts were left substantially as written. The result is that there are some points of overlap; although, given that we sat next to each other for the entire series and constantly chatted about events on and off the field, the surprise is perhaps that there are not many more.

As part of our coverage of each Test we have provided scorecards and splits (for lunch, tea and close of play) as points of reference, and we have appended series averages at the end of the book. Otherwise, what follows comprises daily impressions of the 1997 Ashes series from the rival partisan perspectives of an Australia and an England supporter, and some related matter that was passing back and forth between them. For all six Tests, Norman Geras's account comes first, headed by a Roman I, and Ian Holliday's second, headed by a Roman II. The accounts of each may also be identified by the different styles of designating each successive day's play: as, respectively, 'First Day' and 'Thursday', and so on.

Tentatively and uncertainly begun, this book became for us a labour of love in which both aspects of the phrase were equally prominent. It was once said by a more experienced writer about cricket that producing an account of a Test series is hard work, and so it has been. But we derived enormous pleasure from doing it, and doing it probably influenced how we watched this latest episode of an old and thrilling contest. We hope some of the enjoyment we have had in both the watching and the recording may be shared, through the pages that follow, with others.

Norman Geras
Ian Holliday

August 1997

First Test
Edgbaston
5-8 June

Scorecard

Australia

*M A Taylor c Butcher b Malcolm	7	(2)	c & b Croft		129
M T G Elliott b Gough	6	(1)	b Croft		66
G S Blewett c Hussain b Gough	7		c Butcher b Croft		125
M E Waugh b Gough	5	(6)	c Stewart b Gough		1
S R Waugh c Stewart b Caddick	12	(4)	lbw b Gough		33
M G Bevan c Ealham b Malcolm	8	(5)	c Hussain b Gough		24
†I A Healy c Stewart b Caddick	0		c Atherton b Ealham		30
J N Gillespie lbw b Caddick	4	(10)	run out		0
S K Warne c Malcolm b Caddick	47	(8)	c & b Ealham		32
M S Kasprowicz c Butcher b Caddick	17	(9)	c Butcher b Ealham		0
G D McGrath not out	1		not out		0
Extras (w 2, nb 2)	4		(b 18, lb 12, w 2, nb 5)		37
Total (31.5 overs)	118		(144.4 overs)		477

Fall of wickets 11, 15, 26, 28, 48, 48, 48, 54, 110

133, 327, 354, 393, 399, 431, 465, 465, 477

Bowling *First Innings* Gough 10-1-43-3; Malcolm 10-2-25-2; Caddick 11.5-1-50-5 *Second Innings* Gough 35-7-123-3; Malcolm 21-6-52-0; Croft 43-10-125-3; Caddick 30-6-87-0; Ealham 15.4-3-60-3

England

M A Butcher c Healy b Kasprowicz	8	lbw b Kasprowicz	14
*M A Atherton c Healy b McGrath	2	not out	57
†A J Stewart c Elliott b Gillespie	18	not out	40
N Hussain c Healy b Warne	207		
G P Thorpe c Bevan b McGrath	138		
J P Crawley c Healy b Kasprowicz	1		
M A Ealham not out	53		
R D B Croft c Healy b Kasprowicz	24		
D Gough c Healy b Kasprowicz	0		
A R Caddick lbw b Bevan	0		
Extras (b 4, lb 7, w 1, nb 15)	27	(b 4, lb 4)	8
Total (for 9 dec, 138.4 overs)	478	(for 1, 21.3 overs)	119

Fall of wickets 8, 16, 50, 338, 345, 416, 460, 463, 478

29

Did not bat D E Malcolm

Bowling *First Innings* McGrath 32-8-107-2; Kasprowicz 39-8-113-4; Gillespie 10-1-48-1; Warne 35-8-110-1; Bevan 10.4-0-44-1; S R Waugh 12-2-45-0 *Second Innings* McGrath 7-1-42-0; Kasprowicz 7-0-42-1; Warne 7.3-0-27-0

England won by 9 wickets
Umpires P Willey and S A Bucknor
Toss Australia

Splits

		Lunch	Tea	Close
First day	Australia	92-8	118	
	England		74-3	200-3
Second day	England	335-3	418-6	449-6
Third day	England	478-9 dec		
	Australia	51-0	133-1	256-1
Fourth day	Australia	352-2	403-5	477
	England			119-1

I

First Day

The beginning of an Ashes series. And not just any Ashes series but one which I shall be attending every day of. It's something I've long wanted to do, and Ian and I have had it planned for months. The arrangements are made, the tickets all bought. For Lord's, where tickets are rationed, we even had to write making a special plea, explaining our grand plan to be present at the entire series. Fortunately for us the MCC Secretary obliged.

Anyway, the start of another series between the old adversaries. In a characteristically engaging article in the *Guardian* the day before this Test, Matthew Engel wrote, 'at Edgbaston come 11am tomorrow there will be a sense of expectancy rivalled by nothing else in sport'. That sense of expectancy had certainly taken hold of me as I travelled from Manchester to Birmingham, and as I approached the ground and took my seat. It's not just the special nature of the series from my own point of view. The Ashes is a sporting event to which each of us brings some part of a long history. We watch this match, this series, in the light of others we have followed, from close up or afar. Some of us also bring to it things that go a longer way back: ancient battles, heroic feats, last ditch stands, other dramas.

In my own case the beginning is, dimly, 1954-55, and then, more clearly, 1956. Tyson and Statham followed by Laker, Old Trafford and all that. But I have always supported Australia, and so that glory year of English cricket, 1956, was not at all to my liking. Why Australia? I am not Australian and I've never even visited the country. However, growing up in Southern Rhodesia as it then was, a colony, I started out my cricketing life with a solidarity amongst colonials, and it is something I have never lost, even though I've been in England now for going on 35 years. From the beginning, too, I knew about Bradman, through reading, and he captured my imagination. And then, of course, there was 1956 itself, something to make any Australia-leaning newcomer to the event thirst for revenge. 19 wickets indeed, but that pitch at Old Trafford. (The ground is now a short journey from my home.) Happily for me, for 'us', things were quickly put right in the following series of 1958-59, when May's team was comprehensively thumped by Benaud's, inaugurating a long period of Australian possession of the famous urn. There was, at the time, some unseemly English moaning about Ian Meckiff's bowling action, but that is what you expect from the English camp.

For me these two series, 1956 and 1958-59, also stamp their mark on the whole magnificent contest in a certain very particular way, and this is that their legacy in my own mind is a contradictory image of extreme Australian vulnerability and, as well, massive superiority. There they go with all that talent – Harvey and Benaud, McDonald and Burke, Miller, Mackay – collapsing ignominiously. This tradition of theirs reaches forward into the future, my future. To 1977 and Greg Chappell's Australians. I remember the day at Old Trafford when Chappell played a superb innings of 112, more than half his side's total, while all around him his team mates fell for more or less inconsiderable scores. And then, the mother and father of all ignominies, 1981, summer of Botham, summer of misery. And 1985: crushed again despite a good victory at Lord's. And 1986-87. A whole decade of English victory – with only one or two short Australian interruptions – and the need for fortitude and more fortitude on my part.

But then again, there is Bradman, Bradman nonpareil, whom the Poms have always somewhat resented even while admiring and honouring him. He was a bit too bloody good, a bit too ruthless. So you get the fairy stories about how Jack Hobbs was perhaps the better batsman when all is said and done. As if. Just look at the one unanswerable statistic: 'Bradman... then daylight,' as a recent Australian publication puts it. This refers to the fact that the man had a Test batting average of 99.94 where only a handful of others have made it even into the low 60s, and most of the best batsmen in world cricket are to be found in the upper 40s and the 50s. Then after Bradman, there is, for me, 1958-59: when May wins the toss and inserts the Aussies and he gets hammered, and then Benaud does the same to the English the very next Test and bingo. It ends at 4-0. And then 1974-75 and Lillee and Thommo, and if the first don't get you then the second must. And, sweetest of all, 1989 to 1994-95 inclusive. Massive superiority. Crushing great scores, 600-and-odd for a few declared. Border, Boon, Steve Waugh, Mark Taylor and more, rolling out the hundreds, batting to eternity. One series Terry Alderman and the corridor of uncertainty and just about everybody, but especially Gooch, leg before wicket. Another series Shane Warne and the Ball from Hell. After a wretched period through the late 1970s and the 1980s, how I have enjoyed all this. Can it continue?

I arrive at Edgbaston bringing some figures with me to show to Ian. Ian supports England. Fair enough, I suppose, he is English (but still...). Many in the English camp have been feeling pretty cocky lately since England have won the one-day internationals, Mark Taylor's batting form is terrible, and these unofficial world champions, the mighty Australians are looking... well, vulnerable; thus combining neatly the opposing facets of my now long-standing image of them. Therefore my figures for Ian, in the hope of warding off evil forces. 4-0, 14-2, 111-90, 54-35, 55-25. These being, respectively, the score to Australia in the last four Ashes series, the score in Test victories in those same four series, the score in Tests between the two countries since the beginning of time, the score since the end of the Second World War, and finally Mark Taylor's percentage win-rate in Test matches as compared with Michael Atherton's.

We swap greetings (Ian has driven up from London), swap chat and rivalries and side bets. We settle into our seats for the first morning of 'our' Ashes series. What a morning it turns out to be. I thank the cricketing gods that this is happening after a period of Australian dominance. At one point Australia are 54 for 8! A guy behind us says to a friend arriving shortly before lunch, 'You just missed the best session of English cricket since 1981'. Despite the rout, I sort of enjoy the spectacle. Well, you know, I was *there*. Gough, Malcolm and Caddick all bowl well, the first, in particular, hitting the stumps twice. The Australians recover to some minimal kind of respectability, thanks only to a breezy effort by Shane Warne. Ian is just loving it – and also winning most of the side bets. (In this matter, I am confident, I shall return.) In the afternoon it looks, at first, as though England might just follow in Australia's footsteps. They lose Butcher and Atherton quickly, and then Stewart to a rash shot. They are 50 for 3. Better than 54 for 8, but you never know. Thorpe and Hussain put paid to such speculations. Matching each other nearly run for run, Thorpe attacking from the very start, Hussain more hesitant at first but blossoming as the afternoon proceeds, they deal with everything sent down to them and deal out some beautiful strokes, the boundaries following close on one another. The Australian attack looks to hold no terrors at all.

In the same *Guardian* article, Matthew Engel wrote how the first day of an Ashes series can often define the whole summer. Is this, then, how the fates have arranged it for me? I am to sit right through a summer of English triumph? We shall see.

Second Day

On this day England continued to build towards a victory that must now be all but certain, and there wasn't anything much for Australia to be pleased about. To get out of the game with a draw they would need to bat their socks off and receive some help from the weather.

Both Thorpe and Hussain continued their innings through the morning and into the afternoon. I can't recall an occasion when two batsmen ran their scores in tandem for so long during a partnership. Now one (usually Thorpe), now the other, would pull ahead by a few runs, then they'd be back together again. Both players batted beautifully, with a mixture of concentration and controlled aggression that made the Australian bowlers look unmenacing. Warne, in particular, took rather more punishment than he is used to. I thought Thorpe had the edge on Hussain during most of their partnership, with fewer false strokes, but there wasn't much in it and in the end Hussain pulled ahead in runs significantly for the first time and Thorpe was the one to go. He had made 138 and the two of them had added 288 for the fourth wicket, an Ashes record for England, beating the 222 of Wally Hammond and Eddie Paynter at Lord's in 1938.

Hussain then proceeded to his 200. It was a triumphant moment for him and he deserved the warm applause he got. The double century in an Ashes series puts Hussain in very select company amongst English batsmen: Hammond, Hutton, Barrington, Gower, Paynter, RE Foster. Think of some of the names not on that list: Hobbs, May, Cowdrey, Boycott, Gooch. Hussain will cherish it, as all the English supporters did, including Ian, sitting there next to me and pleased as Punch. Even I had to admire the achievement. Hussain was out shortly afterwards, caught by Ian Healy off Shane Warne, Crawley didn't last long and was also caught by Healy (who has already taken four catches in this innings), and Ealham and Croft then put on 30-odd runs without too much discomfort.

With an hour and 20 minutes left for play the rains came. We waited a while but it soon became clear that that would be that for the day. Another day to England. Oh well, today I won the side bets.

Third Day

This was Mark Taylor's day. If ever a batsman and his team needed a hundred, he was the batsman and Australia the team. For Taylor hadn't made a Test fifty in more than a year and there were many Australians, Ian Chappell prominent among them, calling for his head. The old Australian policy of picking your best team and then finding a captain from within it had been temporarily set aside to allow Taylor one or two more chances. But one or two was plainly it, and after the first innings debacle it is hard to see how he could have continued, had there been another personal failure for him.

This was one part of the context, Taylor's battle with his own cricketing demons. The other was the state of the game itself, Australia having a huge mountain to climb if they were to have any chance of saving it. In that situation teams often fall to pieces. And after the calamity of the first innings, who could feel sure that another collapse would not soon be upon them? But Taylor, first with Matthew Elliott, then with Greg Blewett, stuck it out through most of the day, with one or two interruptions for rain, to recover something psychologically important for Australia in this series, even if they do fail to save the game.

The England innings lasted only another 35 minutes or so, three wickets falling quickly before Atherton declared. Healy took two further catches, to finish with six in the innings, and Michael Kasprowicz, who had stuck well to the task in difficult times, had the best bowling analysis with 4 for 113.

Taylor and Elliott now came to the wicket, with a strong sense of anticipation all round the ground. A Saturday crowd was looking for quick wickets and possibly even an England victory today. The spirit of 1981 many were doubtless hoping had returned, spirit of vertiginous Australian collapse. Just to add to the pressure, Mark Waugh, it had been announced during the morning, was ill and being kept in hospital another 24 hours for observation. I feared the worst. In hope that the *very* worst would not occur, I put Australia's innings total at 260, against Ian's 230, in one of our regular side bets.

But the collapse never came, not today anyway. Taylor and Elliott batted solidly, with the occasional piece of luck to be sure but with some pretty shots as well, and they took Australia past 50, then past 100, with the partnership intact. Taylor brought up his own 50 in 69 balls, including one six. Eventually Elliott was bowled by

Croft, who had forced both batsmen to play with extreme care, and Australia were 133 for 1.

Perhaps this was it, I worried, the gate open for an easy England victory after early resistance. But no. Blewett took up where Elliott left off, and he seemed to play with relative comfort. Taylor, by contrast, after reaching 60, went into a long period of difficulty. His runs now came slowly, he played and missed a lot, edged through the slips, or made to stroke the ball in one direction to find it flying off in another. It was as though during the first part of his innings he had overcome the doubts tormenting him, only to rediscover them later. In moving from 80 to 89, so a guy next to me said, Taylor took 45 minutes. Still, he battled and persisted, crept up towards the century, and finally he got there. It was a triumph of determination and effort and character, less elegant to watch than Hussain's of the previous two days, but in all the circumstances surrounding it no less impressive for all that. It is one of the joys of Test cricket: in the unfolding and the long duration of the game, and whether with or against its prevailing tendency, the drama of the individual's situation.

Taylor has cemented his place in the team and, whatever now happens in this match, he has already ensured that a different cricketing logic will preside over the beginning of the Lord's Test than the one that would have followed a second abject Australian failure.

The day was interrupted by showers, but with both lunch and tea being taken early and the hour added on at the end of the day for time lost, the spectators got full value for their money. There is something deeply wonderful about sitting day after day at good cricket. This despite the oafs and buffoons whose drunken noise is a constant background. You look at the cricket, the state of the match, the personal battles and team crises, the episodes of tension and episodes of ease. You watch the changing cloud patterns, the sun coming and going, the birds. At one point, three of them flying in tight, but gradually changing, formation; at another, one floating up on the wind. It struck me how rarely I see this and the beauty there is in it. While I watch cricket, it is cricket and the environment of cricket that preoccupy me. Much else, the concerns of every day – especially work – I think about not at all.

Fourth Day

In the end the mountain was too high. Australia climbed half way up it, perhaps a stretch more than half way, but then they faltered. England were ready to take their chance and won decisively. I wonder when a team that has scored as much as 477 in either innings last lost by as great a margin as 9 wickets. In any event the game was won and lost on the first morning, as it had seemed to be. Australia's fight-back in their second innings was resolute enough to plant a question mark in our minds as to whether the game might be saved after all despite that catastrophic beginning. But they had too much to do.

For the morning session of this fourth day, things continued Australia's way, with 96 being added for the loss only of Mark Taylor, caught and bowled by Croft for 129. But the second wicket partnership between Taylor and Blewett, worth 194 after that of 133 for the first wicket, was the last really big partnership of the innings. Despite Blewett himself completing a fine century to follow those of Thorpe, Hussain and Taylor, there was now a more or less steady fall of wickets. The later stages of Blewett's innings were marked by half a dozen or more flowing, handsome boundaries on both sides of the wicket, but after he went for 125 it soon became clear the game was up. Croft, Gough and Ealham claimed three wickets apiece, Mark Waugh – back from hospital but whether well again or not we weren't told – came and went, and Gillespie, batting with Michael Bevan as a runner, was run out because this runner failed to attend to the single matter he was there to attend to. Shane Warne once more offered some brief, spirited resistance in the company of Ian Healy, but with the latter's departure there was a speedy denouement, the last four wickets falling in the space of only 12 runs.

The game now had a nice symmetry about it. Australia's second innings score being one short of England's first innings score, to win the match England had to make exactly 118, Australia's first day total. They had 24 overs to do so without going into the final day, but they needed just 21.3. Atherton made an aggressive half-century and England lost only Butcher's wicket. McGrath spilled a hard chance at long leg, but it couldn't have made any difference.

So England are now one up, Ian is pleased and I'm disappointed, though not nearly as crestfallen after Australia's showing in the second innings as I would have been had they completely folded up. In that case I think I might have been ready to kiss the series goodbye. As it is I believe we may still have a contest ahead, though if I were to bet now according to my judgement rather than my loyalties and hopes, I would bet on England recovering the Ashes. The principal reason for this is Australia's bowling. I wonder whether their resources in this department are fully adequate to the task. Their batting is plainly strong but then so is England's; and England's attack in this match seemed much better balanced and more convincing. Anyway it is now to Lord's, where the Poms haven't won since 1934, but that is one kind of record to which I attach no weight at all.

This was a fine Test match, despite the result. It had a spectacular batting collapse, four splendid individual performances with the bat, good bowling from England, most especially Darren Gough, some of the ebb and flow of a well-fought contest and good weather, with just over an hour all told lost to rain, the rest of the interruptions clawed back by the extension of play to seven o'clock.

During the last interruption, while the ground staff were at work clearing up, I walked right around the ground. I have to say, Edgbaston doesn't much impress me as a Test venue. It has not the character of most of the others. And I have also to revise what I wrote yesterday about a cricket ground being a great place to be despite the oafs and buffoons. After our last day's experience here, the qualification is necessary that it depends which oafs, how loathsome they make themselves and how near to you they are. On this occasion our afternoon was spoiled by a group of some dozen or so drunken, loud- and foul-mouthed idiots who scarcely let up over several hours. This was not the more or less good-natured chanting that is part and parcel of watching both cricket and football these days and compatible with actually watching the game absorbedly. It was persistent, ugly, and intrusive upon the attention of anyone trying to focus on the field of play. Why it is tolerated so readily by those in charge of the sport is beyond me. The plea will be, there is nothing they can do. I do not believe that. They could eject people from the ground – steadily, all day. They could encourage amongst the rest of the spectators a culture of opposition to this sort of behaviour. In the end they will have to do something as it gets worse and worse.

The side bet situation is that, after taking an early lead which was then wiped out by my good showing in the middle of the game, Ian just edged ahead in the final innings thanks to Michael Atherton.

I am in debt to the tune of 50p. In this contest, however, I am calmly expecting victory.

And in the other one? Cricket, lovely cricket. Stuff the Poms. 4-0, 14-...er 3, 111-91, 54-36.

II

Thursday

Summer with Norman to follow England's latest attempt to regain the Ashes lost to Australia in 1989. The enterprise seemed uniquely ill-chosen. In a sporting rivalry lasting at least five years, I had known nothing but defeat, Norm nothing but triumph. In football, a string of successes for his Manchester United – including the double double inspired by Eric Cantona – to set against consistent mediocrity on the part of my Tottenham Hotspur. In cricket, an unofficial – but universally acknowledged – world championship for his Australia to set against humiliation by many sides (and particularly Australia) for my England. Now this: a summer which after England's 3-0 victory in the one-day internationals offered the possibility of English revival, the sure-fire certainty of Australian resilience and resistance, and the strong probability that the Ashes would return safely to Australia at the end of the series. I must have been insane to agree to witness every delivery.

True to form, Norm was not about to let our differential recent fortunes escape my notice. As we waited at Edgbaston for the first day's play to begin, he reached into his pocket, took out and unfolded a sheet of paper, and handed it to me. 'Some statistics: 4-0, 14-2, 111-90, 54-35, 55-25.' He'd done this sort of thing before. 2-1-1-2-1-1 at the end of the football season was, for example, United's finishing position in the Premiership from 1992 to 1997. I should, therefore, have been able to figure out this latest set of numbers, but failed to. Maybe I simply chose not to think my way through them. Norm therefore explained them to me. 4-0: Australia's recent record of series victories. 14-2: Australia's record of match victories in those series. 111-90: Australia's lead in all Tests played against England. 54-35: Australia's lead in post-war Tests played against England. 55-25: Mark Taylor's and Michael Atherton's victory percentages as captain. 'Just to put things in perspective Ian. Even if England win 6-0 it'll still be 111-96 to Oz!' Fair enough, but I already knew it was going to be a tough summer.

We settled to taking in the place, which neither of us knew. Edgbaston looked a picture. But on closer inspection it became clear that this impression was generated more by the weather, which was glorious, and the occasion, which could not be other than special, than by the ground itself. Edgbaston is, in fact, a hugely unimpressive Test match venue: a portacabin of a pavilion, a stand which looks as if it was shipped in second-hand from Aston Villa or Birmingham City, and scoreboards which barely convey the basics. Later in the day we discovered that the public address system had been built to match. Only minimal information was ever transmitted by it. No matter. This was the first morning of the first Test, and the sense of expectation was palpable.

Norm and I had, however, important business to transact before the main event got under way. What system of side bets would we run serially throughout the summer? We settled on three categories which could be used in each innings: top scorer, top wicket-taker and team score. (We also recognised that the first two categories could result in no result.) We then fixed the standard bet on each category. Sure, 50p a shot was sufficient. After all, if one of us won every bet throughout the summer, the total debt could amount to £36! (But then how likely was *that*?) Anyway, that was the way it was to be. We agreed, finally, that Norm would take first stab at Australian innings and that I would lead off in English. Would this generate a systematic advantage for one or the other? We thought not. Besides, by this stage in the proceedings Mark Taylor (who had won the toss) and Matthew Elliott were coming out to open the Australian innings. It was time to get down to proper business. Norm: Mark Waugh, Darren Gough, 290. Ian: Taylor, Andrew Caddick, 265. That was nearly that, except that midway through the Australian innings we agreed that an extra 50p would be awarded when a team total fell within a 10-run range of the estimated total, and set the condition that the second guesser could not place himself within 5 runs of the first. We had to cover all the angles. The big bet – of £5 on the series outcome – could not be placed as we both opted for 3-1 to Australia. 'I can't believe you're not going for an England victory!' remonstrated Norm. In my heart, yes. But, as I have already said, in my head I figured from the outset that it would be tough going this summer.

In any context, the first morning of the first day would have been sensational. In this? It was as much as I could do to convince myself that seeing had to be believing. Australia 92 for 8 at lunch does not come close to capturing the drama of the occasion. At one stage – I know this because it stayed for some time on the scoreboard as the last wicket to have fallen – the Australians were 54 for 8. Incredible! Norm of course experienced rather different emotions from mine. At 48 for 7 he was searching the record books for lowest-ever Ashes totals. Australia 58 all out in Brisbane 1936 was the least bad entry in the official tour guide. He immediately set an initial target of 59 for Taylor's team. That at least would limit the humiliation. Taylor himself, though second out for 7, stayed on our list as potential equal top scorer for nearly half the Australian innings. Would I win 50p for that? We hadn't agreed a policy on equal top scorer by the time Steve Waugh moved ahead of Taylor to undermine the debate, at least for the time being. Besides, there was the sheer exhilaration of the England performance to enjoy. The thrill of Gough's early wickets was immense. I know he bowled Mark Waugh after having had him caught off a no-ball the previous delivery. But did he also have Greg Blewett caught in the slips after seeing the previous ball fly through the slip cordon? Or was that Elliott (who was bowled)? It all went by too quickly to tell the full story of 3 for 43 in 10 overs. Devon Malcolm also bowled well. Hostile, controlled and highly effective, he took 2 for 25 in 10 overs. And then Caddick came on to clean up with 5 for 50 in 11.5 overs, and give me one 50p for best bowler and another for team total. It's true that my guess of 265 was miles away from the Australians' final total of 118, but it was closer than Norm's 290. Neither of us had picked Shane Warne as top scorer. Who would have? Just before lunch the guy sitting in the row in front of us – and therefore having to listen to all that passed between us – handed us a *Racing Post* which showed that Warne had been quoted at 100 to 1 for this feat before play began.

It was all a dream; I could think of no other way to describe it. 'Nightmare!' said Norm. Either way, both of us found it hard to believe what was taking place before us. 'Have I missed anything?' asked an Englishman who turned up just before lunch. 'Only the best session in Test cricket since 1981!' We took to debating how this could have happened. The wicket? Possible, the previous two Tests at Edgbaston both having finished inside three days. Australian morale? Also possible, Taylor's captaincy having been the focus of much press speculation in the lead-up to the match following a run of very poor form. English morale? Again possible, the one-day internationals having been won in some style. It was very hard to say.

The plausibility of the wicket theory increased when in the England reply Michael Atherton was out for 2, Mark Butcher for 8 and Alec Stewart for 18, leaving England 50 for 3. Then, however, the match moved into its next incarnation as Nasser Hussain and Graham Thorpe – both playing beautifully (at least by the close in Hussain's case) – took England to 200 for 3 by stumps. 200 for 3! How long could this last? And would Norm win back the money I had secured from him in the first innings with choices of Thorpe, Jason Gillespie and 240 against my Atherton, Glenn McGrath and 195? The bowlers had a wicket each, but on the other two counts I was finished. In fact, I was pretty much done in on all counts, as were all others present from what I could see. Muted jubilation from England fans. After all, who knew what horrors lay ahead? Matching measured despondency from Australia fans. And a strong and defiant sense of history. As one Aussie sitting near us put it in response to English taunts, 'You've only beaten us twice in 10 years!'

Friday

Grey skies over Edgbaston. It seemed unlikely that even Norm's umbrella, initially forgotten but hurried back for, would be able to hold off the rain for the entire day. We settled to the morning papers, using them to impose some sort of order on the events of the first day, and in particular the first session. Three Australian wickets had fallen on 48, something neither Norm nor I had noted despite two wickets in two balls for Caddick. In the period from 12.20 to 12.36 the Australians had slumped from 48 for 4 to 54 for 8. It had all been too much for us to take in fully. Only in the comparative calm of a ninth-wicket partnership of 56 between Shane Warne (47) and Michael Kasprowicz (17) had things seemed clear. Ian Chappell, writing in the *Daily Telegraph*, had the best one-liner: 'Shane Warne dominated the first session for Australia at Edgbaston'. He also restated his by now familiar argument that

Taylor must go. Many journalists noted that English national teams in cricket, football and rugby had experienced a run of recent success that must surely have something to do with the election of Tony Blair's Labour government on 1 May.

Drizzle for the first hour of play did not prevent Hussain and Thorpe from adding 81 runs in 16 overs and taking the game further from Australia's grasp. Norm conjured up his more occult powers to bring the cricketing gods on side. Hussain on 87 with 61 overs bowled surely had to go. 87 for reasons known to all Australians (but few others). 61 because at the first Test Norm had ever watched – South Africa versus England in Johannesburg during the 1956-57 tour – the seemingly invincible Peter May had been dismissed for this score in a game South Africa went on to win. In Birmingham 1997, however, both Hussain and Thorpe pressed on regardless. In the 120s each passed his own highest Test score. With their partnership in the 220s they established a new English record for the fourth wicket against Australia. (It seemed strange that the 222 put together by Walter Hammond and Eddie Paynter at Lord's in 1938 had survived for so long.) None of these milestones being marked by the public address system till lunch-time, we carefully figured them out for ourselves. England 335 for 3 at lunch. Australia quoted by Ladbrokes' stand on the ground at 100 to 1 to win. The dream continued.

Even when Thorpe was dismissed soon after lunch for 138, Hussain batted imperiously on to 207. 50p therefore not won by Norm, and a magnificent innings to boot. Hussain probably hadn't looked so good at the start. Norm said as much. And Thorpe had undeniably looked very assured throughout. But once Hussain got into his stride there was no stopping him, and on the second day he batted beautifully. He moved from 188 to 200 by stroking three glorious fours. The 207 for which Hussain was finally dismissed – caught Healy bowled Warne after 439 minutes, 336 balls and fully 38 fours – turned out to be the highest score of his career.

After Hussain had gone, some of the thrill undeniably went out of proceedings. Mark Ealham chipped in 32 and Robert Croft 18 undefeated runs, but the spell from 416 for 6 (Hussain's dismissal) to 449 for 6 (what turned out to be close of play) was the first passage to be less than wholly enthralling. After tea we turned to debating whether Atherton would declare around 5.00 to give England an hour before stumps to bowl at the Australians. Rain rendered that debate academic. Drizzly from 4.30, it became increasingly heavy from 4.40. We hung around for half an hour until it was clear no more play would be possible in the day.

Saturday

More grey skies over Edgbaston, some of them rain-bearing. But also bright sunshine and virtually clear blue skies for large stretches. Norm cited Bob Hope's 'all four seasons in one day' quip about the English weather, but on the third day of the first Test those four seasons were telescoped into single sessions. Still, the five minutes lost to rain immediately before lunch, the hour lost after lunch, and the few minutes lost around tea were all gathered into rescheduled lunch and tea intervals and the extra hour. The day ended up running precisely to its proper extent, with the final over bowled as 7.00 ticked around. 3-0 to us against the weather as Norm – in keeping with his practice of the first two days – might have said, but didn't.

The morning saw England add a further 28 for 3 in 35 minutes before declaring at 478 for 9. More runs from Ealham, who scored an undefeated 53, and a couple more wickets for Kasprowicz, giving him best bowling figures for the Australians of 4 for 113. The central interest was, however, Ian Healy's growing total of dismissals behind the wicket, watched closely by Norm from the early stage in the innings when Healy snapped up both England openers. Six was the final tally. An Ashes record? The announcer seemed to say as much, but over the Edgbaston system it was never easy to be sure.

The time had come for Australia – and Taylor in particular – to face the music again. A second failure must surely mean the end of Taylor's captaincy and just possibly of his Test career. In a game of high drama, the early stages of the Australian second innings were not surpassed for tension. Norm certainly felt it in every part of his being. He looked on aghast as deliveries whistled past the outside edge of Taylor's bat. 'Jesus, this guy just doesn't know what's happening!' He feared for his captain when England's best strike bowler roared in. 'Gough'll get him.' He saw no grounds for hope. 'This is not a batsman who's going to make runs.' In the event, however, Taylor did: 108 by the close in an innings marked by heebie-jeebies at the start and for most of the period from 61 – the May curse kicking in again – to 89 (inclusive), but characterised throughout by immense tenacity and skill. The extent of playing and missing conjured images of England's inimitable Graeme Fowler, though this century was vastly more substantial than any Fowler ever made. First time past 50 in more than 20 innings. First time past 100 in more than 20 months. Australia out for the count at 360 behind and the guy manages *that*! Even I was rooting for him by the time he reached the 90s, and not only because he was (again) my choice as top scorer. (Norm: Mark Waugh – quickly changed to Blewett when Waugh was reported to be hospitalised with a mysterious illness – Gough, 260. Ian: Taylor, Malcolm, 230.)

Our other major interest revolved around Australian progress towards a notional 600 established by Norm as a match-saving (possibly match-winning) total. At 6 for 0: 'One per cent – ha!' Then 'Two per cent Ian!' And so it continued. By the close the Australians – on 256 for 1 – were well over 40 per cent of the way to 600, Elliott having contributed an excellent but overshadowed 66 and Blewett having made his mark with an undefeated 61. It was undeniably an impressive performance and scorecard, leaving Australia in the comparatively healthy but still (paradoxically) perilous position of minus 104 for 1. Once again this game was threatening to surpass greatest expectations.

Sunday

The match was clearly poised for a thrilling finish, but Edgbaston was no more than half full by the time the fourth day's play commenced at 11.00. At no point during the day did the ground fill completely. Truly this was an odd Test venue. The fourth day was also the most raucous, with divisions of England's Barmy Army quitting the Hollies Stand to which they had been confined during the first three sell-out days and joining us in the Wyatt Stand. From mid-afternoon onwards we were treated to endless rounds of 'Doing the Gladstone Small' (to the tune of 'Doing the Lambeth walk'), 'Atherton's the captain, he wears the captain's hat' ('My old man's a dustman'), 'One man went to bed, went to bed with Shane Warne' ('One man went to mow') and other (often more vulgar) contemporary cricketing classics. The stewards intervened on occasion, but never to any effect. By contrast, the police now and then escorted from the ground men who appeared to have uttered no more than the odd inoffensive slogan. They also dealt with the streakers who took to invading the pitch in the final session, but, we thought, could impose no real penalty on them. By close of play Norm was moving into string-'em-up mode.

On the field Australia initially took up where they had left off. We bet on revised Australian second-innings totals – 390 for Norm, 336 for me – but both were exceeded. The previous day's first-wicket Taylor-Blewett partnership of 133 was also overshadowed by a Taylor-Blewett stand of 194 for the second wicket. After that, however, England just did enough at all the crucial stages to bring the match back within their grasp. I didn't realise it at the time, but the England attack actually took the last nine Australian wickets for 150 to set up what turned out to be a winning position. Indeed, as the day unfolded it did not always seem to me that this was at all what was happening. Equally, Norm was pretty fatalistic throughout. '411 for 5 and still staring defeat in the face!' In the event he was right. 465 for 6 was transformed into 477 all out – just one run short of the England first innings total – by the return of Ealham for a short spell in which rank bad balls were either sent crashing to the boundary by Warne or clipped into a close fielder's hands by the rest of the Australian tail. It was like the 1980s all over again: 'And that's another *appalling* long hop from Botham... He's out!' The wicket which did not fall to Ealham saw Michael Bevan, on as runner for the hamstrung Gillespie, idly stand and watch at square leg as Warne came tearing down the pitch in search of a quick single. Only when it was too late did Bevan twig that he was still a key participant in the game.

Australia one run short of England's first innings total meant that England in their second innings had to match the Australian first innings total to win. 118 in 24 overs was the target. Between innings we took to pondering our chances of getting home that evening and, indeed, whether we would stay an extra night to watch, say, 10 runs being knocked off in the morning. I've got a feeling we would not have done it. We also had to set new conditions for one of our recurrent bets. It was no good estimating the innings total, so we opted instead for wickets lost in getting there. Ian: Atherton, Warne, 4 wickets down. Norm: Stewart, McGrath, 3 wickets down. The only 50p won was mine on Atherton: 57 not out at the close against Stewart's 40 not out. Only Butcher had gone, for 14, with the England score on 29. It was not a trouble-free final phase of the game, but in taking an aggressive approach to wrapping things up

Atherton and Stewart again stamped England's authority on the series. A nine-wicket victory: it seemed about right to me.

Norm was not too despondent, and after such a long run of Australian success I could understand why. He had also had a few days to get used to the idea of an England victory. On the third morning he had even told his daughter Jenny – in London – not to bring her lucky stone to bear on proceedings. Its powers should be reserved for an occasion on which it would stand a chance of making a difference. On the fourth day he toyed with the idea of not applying the sunblock he had used on the first morning and had renounced ever since. But then, on the feeble pretext that he was now wearing a different hat, he went ahead regardless. The guy had given up on Australia's chances long before the finish.

With an England victory behind us we finally placed series side bets on the way home. Ian: 3-1 to England (whilst confessing that 2-2 seemed more likely). Norm: 2-1 to Australia (whilst holding 3-0 to England to be more probable). A fiver each on winning team and margin.

Second Test
Lord's
19-23 June

Scorecard

England

M A Butcher c Blewett b McGrath	5	b Warne	87
*M A Atherton c Taylor b McGrath	1	hit wkt b Kasprowicz	77
†A J Stewart b McGrath	1	c Kasprowicz b McGrath	13
N Hussain lbw b McGrath	19	c & b Warne	0
G P Thorpe c Blewett b Reiffel	21	not out	30
J P Crawley c Healy b McGrath	1	not out	29
M A Ealham c Elliott b Reiffel	7		
R D B Croft c Healy b McGrath	2		
D Gough c Healy b McGrath	10		
A R Caddick lbw b McGrath	1		
D E Malcolm not out	0		
Extras (b 4, nb 5)	9	(b 8, lb 14, w 1, nb 7)	30
Total (42.3 overs)	77	(for 4 dec, 79 overs)	266

Fall of wickets 11, 12, 13, 47, 56, 62, 66, 76, 77

162, 189, 197, 202

Bowling *First Innings* McGrath 20.3-8-38-8; Reiffel 15-9-17-2; Kasprowicz 5-1-9-0; Warne 2-0-9-0 *Second Innings* McGrath 20-5-65-1; Reiffel 13-5-29-0; Kasprowicz 15-3-54-1; Warne 19-4-47-2; Bevan 8-1-29-0; S R Waugh 4-0-20-0

Australia

*M A Taylor b Gough	1
M T G Elliott c Crawley b Caddick	112
G S Blewett c Hussain b Croft	45
M E Waugh c Malcolm b Caddick	33
S K Warne c Hussain b Gough	0
S R Waugh lbw b Caddick	0
M G Bevan c Stewart b Caddick	4
†I A Healy not out	13
P R Reiffel not out	1
Extras (b 1, lb 3)	4
Total (for 7 dec, 61 overs)	213

Fall of wickets 4, 73, 147, 147, 147, 159, 212

Did not bat M S Kasprowicz, G D McGrath

Bowling Gough 20-4-82-2; Caddick 22-6-71-4; Malcolm 7-1-26-0; Croft 12-5-30-1

Match drawn
Umpires D R Shepherd and S Venkataraghavan
Toss Australia

Splits

		Lunch	Tea	Close
First day	No play	–	–	–
Second day	England	38-3	–	–
Third day	England	77		
	Australia		70-1	131-2
Fourth day	Australia	–	–	213-7 dec
Fifth day	England	70-0	169-1	266-4 dec

I

Eve of Test

I steal a march, here, on my buddy and co-spectator. I'm sitting on a bench by Westminster Abbey, down the day before the match to see a guy at the Holocaust Educational Trust and to go to the theatre in the evening with Jenny.

My taxi driver this morning was the very same one as picked me up on the morning of the Edgbaston Test and whom I have ridden with again once since then; a cricket lover himself, and by now the two of us are well into swapping views and impressions. I tell him that I hope this coincidence doesn't augur ill for my team, and we then talk of the prospects for Lord's, of cricket he has watched in Pakistan and, at some length, of the great West Indians of the 1980s. Of Viv Richards' stupendous 189 in the one-day international at Old Trafford in 1984, seen by both my taxi driver and me and surely one of the great innings of modern times, albeit played in the not very elevated context of the limited-over bash. Of Gordon Greenidge, on his day one of the most ruthlessly effective destroyers of a bowling attack. Of the beauty and menace of Michael Holding running up to the wicket to bowl. And of Malcolm Marshall, Joel Garner, Larry Gomes and more of this kind. It is a brief but enjoyable journey, reliving good cricket.

Giants in those days. I don't recall where but I once read something to the effect that watching cricket is remembering cricket, and on my way to Lord's I am remembering Lord's. Not Lord's in general but Lord's and me. First time is 1966, the Monday of the Test, when a West Indian friend, Dick Fletcher, and I are sitting at the Nursery End amongst other West Indian supporters – he threatens once or twice to disclose my identity as a white Rhodesian despite my passionate support for the West Indies side – and what we see is Gary Sobers and his cousin David Holford in an unbroken partnership of nearly 200, moving from a perilous 95 for 5 in the West Indian second innings, a mere nine runs ahead of England who have still to bat again, to 288 and safety. (The following day they were to add a further 80-odd before Sobers declared.) Gary Sobers in that year of 1966: one of the immortals at the top of his game, batting, bowling and fielding like a dream. Will there ever be another all-round cricketer as great? Probably there will if cricket continues long enough, but he would not be like Sobers and that is the glory of it.

Then, after a long interlude, 1984, year once more of the West Indians and of their 5-0 'blackwash' of England. I go with Piwi who has loved cricket with me since the two of us were 12 years old, growing up together in Bulawayo. We step out on to the upper tier of the Edrich Stand and – after so long, I'd forgotten – the scene at Lord's, it takes your breath away. The day, if I remember rightly, was even somewhat overcast, but Lord's nevertheless is resplendent, the jewel of English Test match grounds. Play has already begun. Barely have we taken in the scene and before we can reach our seats, Gatting pads up to a ball from Malcolm Marshall and is lbw. Another thing I remember from that same day: Eldine Baptiste runs out Geoff Miller with a phenomenal throw from the very furthest corner of the ground, breaking the wicket directly as poor Miller, innocent of any danger, casually strolls what he thinks is an easy run. And from the same match, though unfortunately after I am already back in Manchester, Greenidge on the final day lays the England bowling to waste, scoring an imperious 214 to turn a seemingly formidable last day winning target into an easy achievement.

Since that occasion in 1984 I have watched some part of seven further Test matches at Lord's: generally a couple of days from each, but in 1993 (and deeply contented) all but the fifth and last. Not all of these have been memorable days. One of them, of England versus the West Indies in 1995, was so unmemorable indeed that I can recall nothing of it. But there have been creditable centuries – by Robin Smith in 1991 against the West Indies, by Saurav Ganguly in 1996 for India – and there was the day in 1994 when South Africa blew England away in the last innings for a meagre total of 99.

Pride of place for me amongst the occasions I have been at Lord's, however, belongs to the last three Ashes Tests of 1985, 1989 and 1993, the occasions most relevant to our subject here. Three England-Australia Tests at Lord's, three consecutive Australian victories. Each one a thing to cherish. 1985, when Allan Border made a towering 196. When his score was 87, Gatting, fielding close to the bat, appeared to catch the ball, but threw it up too quickly and then failed to hold on to it, so allowing Border a second life. 1989, when Steve Waugh made 152 not out and Geoff Lawson, with 74, helped him add 130 for the ninth wicket, turning Australia's first innings lead from a modest into a substantial one. First over of the

England second innings: Gooch lbw bowled Alderman 0. 1993, the best of the bunch: Australia 632 for 4 declared, with hundreds to Taylor and Slater and Boon, 99 to Mark Waugh, and Border failing miserably with 77. England supporters will perhaps remember better than Waugh's 99 before it, Atherton's dismissal, in his case run out, on the same score.

I could do with Australia continuing this fine sequence at Lord's, to level up the series. The weather forecast the day before the match is gloomy.

First Day

Midway between lunch and tea and thus far we have had no play on account of rain. It was bound to happen at some point in the series, I suppose, but what a shame it has to be at Lord's. I held off coming to the ground until lunch-time since the prospects were dismal when I arrived at Baker Street. But by 12.30, camped out at the *New Left Review* offices in Soho, I noticed a certain brightening up outside and I could no longer hold back; I had to be at the scene of any possible action.

I arrive to find that the MCC guys have done us proud. These are the best seats I've had at Lord's (and we have pretty well identical ones for every day), upper tier of the Edrich Stand and as nearly behind the wicket as you want to be, in line with a point between wicket-keeper and first slip for a left-handed batsman. Ian rolls up a few minutes later; he has in fact been at the ground a bit longer than me, ambling around below the while. The weather prospects continuing to look poor, he decides to go off into town to keep his options open for a possible visit to the theatre. I, with greater devotion to the ritual (or just more fearful lest I miss something?), prefer to hang around. I look at the contents of the Lord's shop, eat my sandwiches, then go and sit in the lower tier of the Edrich Stand and continue with my Lord's reminiscences begun the day before. We huddle against the chill, all of us patiently waiting in the hope of at least *some* cricket. Such are the conditions in which I write. In central London earlier how close and sweaty it seemed. But this is the familiar cold of the English cricket ground in midsummer when there is cloud cover, rain about and a stiff breeze. We wait stoically. I scan several of the day's newspapers, the *Independent*, *Times* and

Daily Telegraph (but not my usual *Guardian*, for I do not find one), all abandoned by those who bought them. Play is eventually called off for the day just after 5.00.

A typical Pommy ploy – to sneak a lucky victory and then hide behind the weather.

Second Day

Today the day dawned bright and, after the usual preparations, I hastened to Lord's in a mood of some hope. The morning forecast wasn't great but it looked as though we might get cricket till mid-afternoon and, after yesterday's experience, anything would be welcome. Anything, alas, is what we got.

Walking up from Baker Street station I found an unopened packet of cigarettes on the pavement. Some strange kind of cricketing luck? I decided to give the cigarettes to Ian to dispose of, just to show that I was above such wild superstition. Arriving at our seats a little before him, I admired the brilliance of the vantage point once again and observed Atherton and Taylor tossing for innings. The word was that Taylor was asking England to bat. All right. I prefer to watch Australia batting, but the conditions look difficult with the cloud cover and all, as Ian points out when he arrives just in the nick of time, with no more than 20 minutes before play is due to start. Side bet time again. He takes Reiffel, who would have been my choice, and so I stick with McGrath. And I decide to bet confidently rather than with my more usual pessimism: I go for England 188 to Ian's 275.

It was a very short day's cricket, just an hour and a half, but it was utterly absorbing and a most encouraging start from Australia's point of view. Conditions indeed proved difficult for batting, with the ball moving about both in the air and off the pitch. McGrath looked an altogether different bowler from the one who had laboured for so little at Edgbaston, and Reiffel, though he claimed no wicket, also bowled well. England, starting quietly, struggled into double figures, Atherton looking reasonably secure but watchful, Butcher as if he was desperately clinging on. A couple of lbw appeals against him couldn't have been missing by much, if in fact they were missing, but it was immaterial. He soon prodded a meek bat-pad catch to Greg Blewett, McGrath had a wicket and England were 11 for 1. In no time it was 13 for 3. Atherton fell for 1, also off McGrath, to a beautifully taken catch at first slip by Mark Taylor, and Stewart misjudged an off-stump delivery, leaving it alone to break his wicket. My 188 was looking good and the Barmy Army, if it was here at all, was mute.

The heroes of Edgbaston, Hussain and Thorpe, now came together again and they too struggled at first. Thorpe was very nearly out edging to Healy, who appeared to scoop the ball into his gloves, with some of the slip cordon going up to claim the catch. David Shepherd was about to confer with the square-leg umpire, Venkat (Srinivasaraghavan Venkataraghavan, Indian off-spinner of the 1970s), when Healy ran over to them to confess he wasn't sure he'd made the catch, an act for which he was applauded by both Shepherd and the crowd (but not the mean-spirited Mike Selvey in next morning's *Guardian*). The sky began to darken at this point as for the first time in the morning the batsmen played some convincing shots. Having taken more than an hour getting to 20, they sped to 38 in a couple of overs. Then the clouds opened and that was that for the day. Ian and I headed off in the direction of the St John's Wood Bridge Club where we spent an expensive afternoon learning the particularities of 'Chicago'.

An hour and a half of cricket was better than no cricket, but with most of two days now lost to rain this game is barely alive, and with more rain forecast for the weekend it could soon be quite dead. Ian and I are discussing whether we would stay for Monday in the circumstances. A difficult one. I see the pointlessness of it on one level. But what about our grand plan? What about completeness? What about the status of our journal of the series – whose prospects we were discussing during Hussain and Thorpe's brief flourish – if we were to miss a day? I am reminded of the time in 1992 when Piwi drove from Hitchin to Manchester to join Morris and Dan and me at the last day of an altogether extinct Test against Pakistan.

Third Day

This was another remarkable day's cricket and it was remarkable aside from the cricket. So far the present series is maintaining the reputation of the Ashes for drama and interest.

I arrived at the ground unusually late for me, with just 10 minutes before play was due to begin, to find Ian already in his seat.

On the way up to Lord's I had phoned Soph and Jen in Cambridge and they told me that Adèle's mother had died. We had been expecting this from some days before, when she had had a stroke after a long period of declining health. Jenny, Soph and Dan were driving up to Manchester the same day to take care of things at home till my return, while Adèle flew to Israel for the funeral. I phoned Adèle to see how she was and to discuss arrangements.

The weather today was kinder to us. We managed, in terms of overs, something like two-thirds of a full day's play. This was the respect, apart from the cricket itself, in which the occasion was remarkable even by the standards of the English game. For there were, if I didn't lose count, *six* interruptions for rain. I have been at Old Trafford when rain claims most of the day. Today, however, was different. There were many short sessions of cricket, and there were many short(ish) sessions of rain in between.

Skywatching. You study the heavens as intensely as you study the game itself, and how they do change. At one moment glorious sunshine, an expanse of blue standing above Lord's, with a thick border of mostly white cloud. Then, wisps floating across the blue. Then, within a matter of moments, it has thickened up, it becomes dark and threatening, some drops are felt on the face and everyone is fossicking with umbrellas and coats or running for cover. Off go the men in white, and then when they return, 10 or 25 or 40 minutes later, the game begins once more. Cricket. Skywatching. Now *this* cloud formation is again different, with the sky as it were split, clear from midway and over to the south, thick and menacing in the other half, over to the north. But given the wind, always brisk, sometimes buffeting, the other half matters less – or so we read things. It will miss us. The better half is our immediate future. We watch and watch, one eye on the ball, the other on the clouds. If you sit, as we do, opposite the Lord's pavilion, there is an airliner all but permanently painted on the sky over to the left and above the pavilion, on a stretch, as we deduce, of the flight path into Heathrow.

Remarkable day, extraordinary cricket. England are bowled out for 77 – 77! – 10 minutes before lunch, losing 7 wickets for 39 where yesterday they lost 3 wickets for 38. Later research reveals that, other than a 52 at the Oval against Bradman's side in 1948, this is England's lowest Ashes total since the early years of the century. I have to say I relish it. It may help to put things back in perspective after Edgbaston. Ian, naturally, is less happy about things but, like me at Edgbaston, he takes it all in good, cricket-loving spirit: the turn of the wheel, spirit of the game and all that. Which is not to say (to keep this in proper proportion) that both of us wouldn't just love to see our own team sticking it to the other's. Anyway, today is Australia's, and my, day. And Glenn McGrath's.

After the micro-recovery by Thorpe and Hussain the previous day, there was nothing to match even that in the rest of the England innings. McGrath bowled superbly, with both speed and accuracy on a difficult wicket, and the batsmen came and went in regular procession: 47 for 4, 56 for 5, 62 for 6 and so on. Only Hussain offered anything like resistance and he was unfortunate in being dismissed lbw first ball after an interruption for rain, the break in concentration obviously not helping him. Gough, in his manner, determined to have a go, and he collected a couple of fours before mis-hitting one high for Healy to take a comfortable catch. In all, Healy accumulated another three England scalps, Reiffel bowled with great economy for his two wickets, but the main story of the day was McGrath's. Resurrected since Edgbaston, he took 8 for 38, bettering both of Bob Massie's eight-wicket hauls on this ground in 1972. It was a wonderful performance.

My optimism in estimating the England total having more than paid off, I decided to repeat it in betting on the Australian one. But on this wicket, in these conditions, what would be a sensible optimism? How far was the 77 due to good bowling or weak batting and how far was it due to the conditions? I go for cautious optimism and I predict 150 to Ian's 112. Taylor is bowled spectacularly, playing on, his middle stump cleanly taken out from between the other two. Australia are 4 for 1. (Taylor, incidentally, is the fifth batsman out of 12 so far to post the score of 1.) We wonder if the Australian innings will just continue the pattern of England's. It doesn't. Blewett and Elliott add 69 and then Elliott and Mark Waugh another 58 unbroken, and with the day ending with Australia on 131, Ian's 112 is already busted. All three of these Australian batsmen have played watchfully, ridden their luck, and chosen the ball to punish, and Elliott has come away with a commendable half-century. Ridden their luck: there have been four clear chances missed. Blewett has been let off because the slips were unable to make up their minds who should be the one to go for the catch; Elliott has been dropped by Malcolm and by Butcher, both chances that would be taken on most other days; and Waugh has been put down by

Hussain. Funny game. At Edgbaston the England fielders would have eaten these for breakfast. But here the wind and the chill. And just possibly a new element of doubt?

In any case we have seen a decent amount of cricket at last. Weather permitting, this game could become very interesting. But how much of anything the weather will permit is likely to be the main question.

Fourth Day

Some good way into the day at Lord's today, a ripple of applause went round the ground. A fine stroke? An impressive piece of fielding? Some amiable display or other, such as has become customary at Test matches during the lunch interval? In fact, appreciation for the heroic efforts of the ground staff, working indefatigably to clear away the water from the field of play even as more of the stuff was falling from the sky. They were finally taking a break. It is a very particular kind of labour, theirs, on a day like this of heavy showers. Methodically, repetitively, they work to undo the effects of the last downpour, in the near certainty, looking up above, that this work will soon be undone by the effects of the next one.

Ian and I waited and watched and read the Sunday newspapers. We talked of this and that, of games we had played and enjoyed, from Scrabble to the ancient oriental game of Go – until at 2.40 we set off again to the St John's Wood Bridge Club where we knew a session of duplicate was about to begin. It was a bad mistake. Watching the rain would have been many times preferable. It was a mistake which, by a rare piece of pre-arrangement in this joint chronicle of ours, I leave it to my co-author to relate.

We returned – at once relieved and contrite – for the resumption of play at 5.40. At last, we calculated, towards the very end of the fourth day of the match, we would pass the 90-over mark, normal ration for a single, normal day. And yet even with the better part of three days lost, if the weather would just butt out of things now, there could still be a lot in this game.

We anyway derived much entertainment from the short session this evening, the more especially after the torment of the bridge club. Australia came out determined to push things along, to the point of foolhardiness in my own view. The wickets of Mark Waugh and Shane Warne were uselessly given away, with soft, lofted catches, and Steve Waugh was trapped lbw first ball, three wickets falling at 147. Bevan too went, caught behind, giving Caddick his third wicket of the innings. Elliott and Healy then steadied things in a brisk half-century partnership. Elliott was now the man: he hit three successive fours off a Darren Gough over costing 15 runs in all, and two more fours off Caddick's next. Suddenly he was in the nineties. He was striking the ball in a bold, but more effective and intelligent, way than either Waugh or Warne and he showed a command of the situation that was invaluable to Australia, every one of his many boundaries immaculate, finding the gaps between the fielders, racing away. He reached his century, the first of his Test career, with a quick single to mid-off off Croft, and in the circumstances of this game so far, it was gold. It earned Elliott a generous ovation from what remained of the Lord's crowd, their admiration for a fine display perhaps mixed, amongst England supporters, with some regret that he hadn't been dismissed on the previous day from the chances he gave. Finally he was, caught in the deep by Crawley, again off Caddick, for 112.

Australia now have an opportunity to win this game, though a draw is surely more likely still. If they could do it, how pleased I'd be. Walking back down to Baker Street I even secured from Ian that, offered the choice between a full day's play on the last day with Australia winning, and another wash-out, he would take the former – at *this* stage of the series anyway. Now there's a love of the game for you.

Fifth Day

On this final day the weather relented, allowing us a normal portion of cricket, and England negotiated their way to a draw. A moderate-sized crowd enjoyed the remainder of the game, charged only a fiver per head. Not for the first time it struck me how strange it is that so few people seem to want to see the last day of a Test match, even with an interesting finish in prospect. To sit at Lord's several hours for as little as £5 is extremely good value. Another feature of today's crowd was the high proportion of Australians it contained. Like me, they were doubtless hoping we might draw level, but it wasn't to be.

For the first session Atherton and Butcher batted with a proper sense of what was at stake, and the only real alarm from an England point of view came when Butcher offered a chance off Reiffel to Taylor at first slip. Taylor failed to make the catch. England were 12 at the time and Butcher had 2. From there he and Atherton moved safely through to lunch with 70 on the board. They continued steadily after that, increasing the run rate a shade. The devil in the wicket, the conditions and the bowling seemed now to have receded or been tamed. I had a bet – with Ladbrokes, not with Ian – on 111-120 runs during the middle session: for £2 and at 9 to 1. To my disappointment I was looking in good shape to win it. But first Atherton stepped back on to his wicket, turning a ball from Kasprowicz to fine leg (Atherton 77, England 162 for 1); and then, at 3.30, 10 minutes early, the weather made one last face at us and forced the players off prematurely for tea. I was only 12 runs away from picking up 18 quid.

After the interval, now too late for Australia, there was a small flurry of wickets, of the sort they could have done with earlier in the day, including two smart dismissals for Shane Warne: a return catch from Hussain, out for 0, and a ball that defeated Butcher, bowling him for 87. Thorpe and Crawley then added an untroubled 64 before play was brought to an end at 5.20, Atherton declaring the innings closed from the England balcony.

Ian and I had been hoping to get the seven o'clock train back to Manchester. We wondered if we might now make the six o'clock instead and decided to go for it. Thirty minutes flat from the top of the Edrich Stand to Euston and on the train with some time to spare – this including a suitcase collected from left luggage, a phone call home and buying a couple of Cokes.

The series is left at 1-0, with all still to play for, but not exactly where things were before. The contest announced by Australia in their second innings at Edgbaston was toughened up some here at Lord's, before England fought back for what Ian and I agree is an honourable draw. For the time being, then, a greater sense of evenness as we await the next development in the plot. And a match with a memorable bowling performance and some memorable weather, too memorable by far.

I decide, on the train home, that Australia and I are on a rising curve, England and Ian on a declining one. Respectively 1-0 and 50p up at the end of the Edgbaston Test, that is where England and he remain after Lord's. I must tell him this.

II

Thursday

Following England's victory at Edgbaston, cricket was back in the national spotlight. By the first day of the second Test, the Ashes series had been built up in the press and the popular imagination to an extent that had few recent parallels. Indeed, had there been this much interest in cricket at any point since 1981? Maybe there had, for England still had no heroes of the stature of Botham and Gower, and both of them played long after that epic Ashes series. But in the 1990s it had been mainly a case of doom and gloom, and that certainly was gone, at least for the time being.

One fact dominated all others reported in the press. It naturally reached me first via Norm. At Edgbaston – perhaps not coincidentally on about the second day when Australia were nowhere in sight and he was clutching for straws of comfort – he set the issue up. 'Do you know when England last beat Australia at Lord's Ian?' I thought for a bit. This clearly wasn't an innocent question. Some time in the 1980s? Impossible. A bit further back? I plumped for the early 1970s. '1930!' said Norm triumphantly. He turned out to be wrong about that – it was actually 1934 – but the essence of what he was saying was spot on. Lord's was not England's lucky ground, though no one could really explain why and even Norm at Edgbaston claimed to have no time for lucky ground statistics anyway. The point was, however, endlessly repeated in the papers. Other factors held to make this a classic encounter were the twenty-fifth anniversary of Bob Massie's debut 16 wickets for not many runs for the Australians in 1972, and Mike Atherton's record forty-second Test as England captain (surpassing the 41 registered by Peter May, who seemed set to haunt this series).

There was, however, also the issue of the weather. At 8.00 on the first morning it was clear from my bed in Islington that cars were splashing through the streets. But was it actually raining? A quick peep between the curtains revealed that it was. I phoned Norm, who was not yet into the day and therefore not yet decided what to do. We fumbled our way to a plan, including fallback. A little later Norm called me. The recorded message at Lord's, timed at 9.25, said that the umpires were also undecided. We firmed up our fallback plan.

As there was no point in going to the ground yet I dropped in on a friend for a chat. It was still pouring as 11.00 ticked around, so there was no need to worry. In central London less than an hour later, however, the skies had cleared, the pavements were drying and cricket looked decidedly possible. I just had time in the National Portrait Gallery to buy, write and send a postcard of Helmut Newton's 1991 portrait of Margaret Thatcher before hurrying by tube to the ground. 12.30 when I got there. I asked a steward for the latest news: no play possible till after lunch at 1.40. I went to our seats at the top, back and extreme right of the Edrich Stand – looking pretty much wicket to wicket from the Nursery End – and had lunch while contemplating the scene. There was a good deal of activity in the middle, with ground staff shifting covers and players poking around. But there were also dark clouds overhead. 'It's going to be touch and go today chaps!' said the old buffer in the row in front. That was the problem. It was very hard to judge things either way. I wandered off to the nets: desultory activity. A bit later I climbed back to the top of the Edrich Stand to find Norm in raptures about our seats but also wondering whether we would ever be able to put them to good use. Spots of rain were in the air by this time. But according to Norm hope lay on the horizon. I tried, unsuccessfully, to locate it.

The time had come to take a decision. *Damn Yankees*, a musical about baseball, the world's other great sport, was on at the Adelphi at 2.30. I was dying to go. I figured I could keep my options open by travelling to the Strand and reassessing things there. I therefore took a pass-out and hurried back to town, getting off the tube at Piccadilly Circus because the Bakerloo line was under repair for the rest of its stretch to the Elephant and Castle. My route to the Strand thus passed the Half Price Ticket Booth in Leicester Square. As the weather was certainly no better I bought a stalls ticket for £13.25, only to find at the theatre that the same seats were on sale for £10. A bad omen? There was no point in thinking about it now. I went to my seat praying for rain (and at the same time apologising to Norm for doing so). Although the show was undeniably superb – the highlight being a 15-minute stand-up routine by Jerry Lewis in the second half – it was difficult to enjoy it fully when there was always a chance that the skies had cleared at Lord's. In fact, was that sunshine pouring into the theatre during the interval? I tried not to look. At the end, to my great relief, I came out to rain. Maybe there had been no cricket after all.

I went to eat, wondering both whether a ball had been bowled at Lord's and who had won the Tory leadership third-round run-off. Kenneth Clarke or William Hague? Clarke's pact with the second-round loser, John Redwood, seemed to make him the favourite. He was also held by the pundits to be the only man with even an outside chance of holding the party together. But with Conservative MPs in such a febrile state the result was very hard to predict.

Back on the streets – where it was still raining – one of my questions was answered when I bumped into Norm's daughter Jenny near Leicester Square tube station. There had definitely been no cricket. Jen also told me that she was now on her third lucky stone, picked from the garden when the second went missing at some critical moment in her life. What sort of a deal was this? Could I not simply discount such evidently arbitrary charms?

My other question was answered when at 7.15 I met Norm at St John's Wood tube station to go to play bridge at the local club. Hague had won by 20 votes (92-70 as it turned out). This was not at all what I had expected. When I mentioned Jen and the lucky stone, Norm also told me he had asked her to bring the stone's powers to bear on the second Test. So was that why there had been no play on the first day? The Aussies were running scared! I tried this on Norm, but for some reason he wouldn't buy it. We took to mulling over our fate. It was all too possible that four days of rain-affected, meaningless cricket lay ahead.

Friday

No sound of puddles in the street. My hopes were confirmed when I ventured out of bed and drew the curtains. Oh what a beautiful morning! There was some cloud cover, but there were also big blue patches and lots of bright light. I trooped down into the underground in good cheer. As I walked the final stretch to Lord's from Baker Street things still looked pretty hopeful. It's true that there was now much more cloud cover, but none of it looked like dumping rain on us for a good while yet. In the ground Norm, already stationed in his seat (of course), told me that the rain was forecast to hold off until at least 4.00. At last watching the game rather than the sky was in prospect. And Norm and I could even turn to laying side bets. Australia had won the toss and put England in. Ian:

Thorpe, Reiffel, 275. Norm: Atherton, McGrath, 188. Paul Reiffel was the only change to either team since Edgbaston, coming in for the injured Jason Gillespie. Ideally suited to English conditions, he seemed a natural choice. Yet he had in fact only joined the Australian party in the past two weeks. Much head-shaking by Norm, who would have bet on him if I hadn't got in first.

Within an hour it looked like I had done him quite a favour. England 13 for 3 was the worst of it, and McGrath had taken all three wickets. 'Edgbaston proportions!' said Norm gleefully, though neither of us could remember the exact course of events there. When *had* the third Australian wicket fallen on the first morning? Norm, naturally, rustled up a scorecard within seconds. But the one he turned to – in the match programme – gave neither fall of wickets nor bowling analyses. 'What kind of a scorecard is that?' asked Norm rhetorically. We turned back to the game. After a little more than an hour, and 16 overs, England were 16 for 3, with McGrath having taken 3 for 9 in 8 overs. Not a bad start for the Australians. Butcher never looked comfortable, and popped up a bat-pad catch for Blewett. Atherton looked entirely comfortable, until he was brilliantly caught inches from the turf by Taylor at what I could have sworn was second slip, but in fact turned out to be first. Stewart was bowled by an absolute beauty which he left only to see come back enough to nick the top of his off stump. This dismissal generated a no-result on one of our ad hoc side bets – introduced by Norm – on the manner of Stewart's dismissal. Norm: lbw. Ian: caught somewhere behind the wicket. I was never entirely sure why this particular issue had come up. To 16 for 3 Butcher had contributed five runs (including a streaky four over the slips), Atherton, Stewart, Hussain and Thorpe one each (the latter two being undefeated), and Extras seven. It was absorbing – if also rather disturbing – cricket, and our view of it was superb.

In the next passage of play England started to fight back. Both Hussain and Thorpe even played a convincing stroke or two. But at 12.30, with England 38 for 3 after 21 overs, the rain came. In no time at all it was pouring. So much for making it through to 4.00. I recalled that in the morning papers I had read that the first day of the second Test was the first time in five years (and the eighty-third time in history) that a whole day's play had been lost to rain in England. It was also the fourth time such an occurrence had come to pass on the opening day of the Lord's Test. But on how many of those occasions had the next day seen rain fall from the skies before even the morning session was complete?

What to do? There were no matinees at all in the West End. A trip to a cinema in town was too big a commitment for Norm. After all, if the rain stopped *now*, who knew how quickly the cricket might resume? A visit to the public library up the road was not in the least bit inviting to either of us. We opted to return to the St John's Wood Bridge Club to seek out a game for the afternoon, and from 3.00 to 5.30 played Chicago with a couple of pensioners for 50p per 100 points. On each occasion that he was dummy Norm called Lord's to confirm what we already knew: no play. But you can never be too careful. It was the first time either of us had played bridge for money, and although we did pretty well to begin with our luck turned at the end and we each came out £16 down on the game, plus £6 each for use of the table. The pensioners had cleaned up. At least the Test match raincheck scheme would cover our losses.

Saturday

I woke to a glorious morning. But by this stage I had no hope whatsoever that the good start would be sustained. The BBC's forecast the previous night had said frequent showers throughout the weekend, some of which would be thundery on Saturday. The simulated satellite picture of the nation at 13.00 on Saturday was a blanket of rain. Summer was said to be nowhere in sight. Sunshine and blue skies could not therefore last.

I started off for the ground all the same, so absorbed in the collapse of Jonathan Aitken's libel action against the *Guardian* and *World in Action* that I did not even get to the cricket reports until I had reached Lord's. 'He lied and lied and lied', screamed the *Guardian* headline. That was the Aitken case in a nutshell. The strange occurrence at the ground was that Norm was not yet there when I showed up at 10.40. Arriving 10 minutes later, he explained that his mother-in-law – in Israel – had died overnight, prompting calls home and elsewhere.

Cricket at 11.00. This was already more than we had dared hope for. Indeed, in the early part of the morning every successive delivery seemed like a generous and entirely unexpected gift from the gods. '18 minutes snatched from the rain!' said Norm a few overs in. At 11.40, when the sun made its first appearance of the match, a burst of applause rippled round the ground. In fact, things turned out pretty well on the weather front. 65 overs in the day was about 65 more than we had thought possible before play started. At times things got difficult. Around 5.00 there was a passage of play in which 11 balls were bowled (and two runs scored) followed by a further three balls (one run scored). But somehow or other we got through the day without any major interruptions. As Norm put it at lunch-time, 'We're hanging in by the skin of our teeth today Ian!' It was hard to picture, but I knew what he meant.

On the cricket front things looked less sunny for me. By close of play the Australians were 131 for 2 in response to England's 77 all out, establishing an unprecedented dominance for them in this series. Was Jenny's stone having an effect after all? The performance of the day, which is certain to be a highlight of the series, was McGrath's haul of 8 for 38 in 20.3 overs in the England innings. The guy was totally transformed from the man who at Edgbaston had trotted in and lobbed medium-pacers in the general direction of the English batsmen. Here at Lord's he was largely unplayable, and certainly treated us to one of the great fast bowling performances. Clearly the conditions were not good for batting, both in the movement offered by the wicket and in the interruptions imposed by rain. Hussain, who looked pretty good for 19 runs, was, for example, out to the first ball after a rain-generated interval. But there was no denying that Australia, and particularly McGrath, had made the best of those conditions. 77 all out was easily sub-Edgbaston.

Strangely, though, things did not strike me as notably disastrous. This must have been because the wicket looked a highly plausible cause of England's humiliation, and could presumably be expected to bring Australia to grief too. It might also have been because at start of play I had persuaded Norm to bet on England lunch-time scores, chiefly because the rain had rather undermined our gambling activity. Ian: 96 for 7. Norm: 115 for 5. 50p each on runs scored and wickets taken. I won on both counts when England's final wicket fell at 12.50, prompting charges from Norm that I'd pulled a dastardly trick on him. Ad hoc bets, he maintained, were in some sense 'inferior' to regular ones. I was not persuaded.

It was, however, time to place new regular bets on the Australian innings. Norm: Steve Waugh, Gough, 150. Ian: Mark Waugh, Malcolm, 112. By close of play it had become clear that we had both overestimated the horrors of the pitch and underestimated the ability of the Australians to exploit a favourable position when it stared them in the face. 131 for 2 at stumps might already be close to a match-winning position. Blewett, playing with fire at times and beautifully at others, had made 45. Both Elliott, on 55, and Mark Waugh, on 26, were undefeated. Only Taylor had failed, with 1. England, it has to be said, did nothing to help their cause by putting down four clear chances in the field.

As we left the ground the state of play seemed a bit unreal to me. Australia were clearly in a great position. But would they be able to turn it into victory? I had not yet given up hope that England could see them off.

Sunday

It was not actually raining when I looked out, but it was certainly on the point of doing so. Sure enough, the heavens opened as I stepped out of the house at 9.45 and obliged me to wait five minutes for the rain to ease off. That, really, was the theme of the first half of the fourth day. At Lord's it was never worse than intermittent showers, but each one was an absolute killer and in a matter of minutes – seconds even – undid the mopping-up activity of the previous hour or two. At one stage we even watched hail stones bounce from the covers. It seemed highly unlikely that we would see any play in the day. We passed the time reading the Sunday papers, watching the sterling efforts of the ground staff, taking an early lunch, walking round the ground and wishing we'd brought a game of Scrabble. The papers revealed that McGrath's 8 for 38 was the best return by an Australian at Lord's, the third best by an Australian ever, and the twenty-fourth best in Test cricket ever. Only Botham has better figures at Lord's.

For Norm and me 3.00 was the critical moment in the day, being the time at which duplicate bridge would start at the club in St John's Wood. We walked over there at 2.40 in another keeping-options-open operation. By 3.00 more rain seemed highly likely to our eyes, by this stage expert, we thought, in weather forecasting. And the next pitch inspection would not even take place till 4.00. We decided, without too much soul-searching, that we would play, aware that we were committing ourselves to a round of duplicate which might not be complete until 6.00. It was a decision we came to regret. From the minute we started to play – in a duplicate competition comprising a mere two and a half tables – the skies began to clear and the ground to dry. The first round of anxiety attacks set in. At 4.00, however, a small amount of rain fell. Relief for Norm and me, though short-lived because it came to nothing. We settled to further bridge, interspersed by Norm's phone calls to the ground and clouded by the second round of anxiety attacks. Sunshine and blue skies were now breaking out all over! When the recorded message at Lord's stated that play would resume at 5.40 unless there was a further deterioration, and when there plainly was none, we simply had to leave. As the duplicate round had not yet finished this felt – and was – bad. We resolved on the short walk to Lord's to send a letter of apology.

It was, however, a huge relief to be back at the ground with a prospect of play. Although Norm was still complaining about the 'easy' side bets I had 'tricked' him into placing on England's score by lunch-time Saturday – runs and wickets – he reluctantly agreed to take a bet on Australian runs scored (but not wickets lost) by close of play, provided I chose first. 231. '231?!' Norm duly raised his bet from 180 to 205, and thereby won when the close of play score turned out to be 213 for 7. Only a brief interruption for rain had denied me yet another 50p. I claimed a moral victory, but Norm was having none of that.

Still, it was an excellent short session. The vast bulk of the Australian runs came from Elliott, who moved from his overnight score of 55 to 112 in the penultimate of 17.4 overs, when he was out hooking Caddick. The power and placement of some of his strokes was superlative, and despite the number of chances he had given (but had not had accepted) on Saturday – three by most counts – this was a very good innings. Before that flurry of activity, the Australians in their run chase lost four wickets for 12, including Warne and Steve Waugh (who came in in that order) for 0 each, as they moved from 147 for 2 to 159 for 6. Dark mutterings from Norm: 'Border would never have let this happen'. If so, Border may well have been mistaken, for by close of play the Australians had added 81 for 5. Their lead now stood at 136, and had surely set up an overnight declaration and a very difficult final day for England. Indeed, although we had only had just over one full day's play in the first four days of the match, Australia were in a potentially winning position. At least a meaningless final day might be avoided. And the stage was perfectly set for a classic Athertonian rearguard action.

Monday

Grey skies, but surely not menacing. As on the second day, I travelled to the ground in hope. A mistake? At 10.20, as I supped tea in a café outside Baker Street station, rain started to fall and umbrellas to go up. In the event my instincts – bolstered by the weather forecast seen by Norm the previous evening – turned out to be correct. A brief shower passed over Lord's at 3.30, prompting an early break for tea, but otherwise it was a clear and dry day. When stumps were drawn at 5.20 – Atherton, it turned out, having declared to save us a final 10 minutes of largely irrelevant cricket – the weather was better than at any time in the match, with sunshine streaming from a bright blue sky.

I guess a draw was always the most likely result, and so it turned out, with England 266 for 4 by the close. But they had to work hard to get there. I took Norm's bets from England's first innings for their second: Atherton, McGrath, 188. Norm took my players from the first innings – Thorpe and Reiffel – but not my score of 275. Instead, he opted for 142, and thereby lost that particular bet. The majority of the salvage operation was undertaken by England's openers, who put on 70 by lunch and were only parted when England had an overall lead of 26 with 162 on the board. Butcher survived an easy chance – to first slip Taylor off Reiffel – on 2, but eventually grew in confidence to reach 87. He hit some very handsome fours towards the end of that innings. Atherton, who looked commanding throughout, was bizarrely out first – for 77 – when he stepped on his wicket while touching a ball from Kasprowicz to fine leg for what should have been a single. In the 1993 Ashes Test at Lord's he had slipped and been run out for 99. Strange goings on. Things then got a little tricky for England as Stewart went for 13, Hussain for 0 and Butcher for his 87 (beautifully bowled by Warne, who was at last making a mark on the series). At no point, however, were they in danger of throwing the match away. The minor collapse from 189 for 1 to 202 for 4 was halted by Thorpe and Crawley, who took some easy runs off a tiring Australian attack in the final overs of the match. They were undefeated on 30 and 29 by the close.

Pondering the day's events in the dressing room, Atherton must have been kicking himself to have missed out on a century, and on the very erratic late bowling of Bevan in particular.

As the match meandered to a close the Barmy Army stirred itself for the first time since Edgbaston and chipped in the odd chant, usually 'One-nil to the Ingerland'. A small band of Australians responded with 'Aussie, Aussie, Aussie, Oi! Oi! Oi!', a refrain to which Norm became fleetingly partial as the afternoon ran its course. But on the whole the match was mercifully free of this kind of disruption, Lord's evidently drawing its customary better class of cricket-watcher.

The second Test thus finished in the only way appropriate to little more than two full days' play. Just over 180 overs were bowled in total, and an entirely honourable draw was played out. Norm and I hurried off to catch the train back to Manchester with England still 1-0 up, me still 50p up on side bets, and the weather having fought back tenaciously from its 4-0 thrashing at Edgbaston. By the end of the Lord's Test we could claim no more than a 6-3 advantage on that front, possibly less. I tried to figure out what all this meant for Norm's raft of superstitions. Also, was he right when we got home to contend that I was on a downward curve, having seen victories for England and myself (on side bets) at Edgbaston turn into draws at Lord's? Or was I right to argue that a lead was a lead, and that he and his team had done nothing to dent England's and mine? That debate would certainly resurface at Old Trafford.

Third Test
Old Trafford
3-7 July

Scorecard

Australia

*M A Taylor c Thorpe b Headley	2	(2)	c Butcher b Headley	1
M T G Elliott c Stewart b Headley	40	(1)	c Butcher b Headley	11
G S Blewett b Gough	8		c Hussain b Croft	19
M E Waugh c Stewart b Ealham	12		b Ealham	55
S R Waugh b Gough	108		c Stewart b Headley	116
M G Bevan c Stewart b Headley	7		c Atherton b Headley	0
†I A Healy c Stewart b Caddick	9		c Butcher b Croft	47
S K Warne c Stewart b Ealham	3		c Stewart b Caddick	53
P R Reiffel b Gough	31		not out	45
J N Gillespie c Stewart b Headley	0		not out	28
G D McGrath not out	0			
Extras (b 8, lb 4, nb 3)	15		(b 1, lb 13, nb 6)	20
Total (77.3 overs)	235		(for 8 dec, 122 overs)	395

Fall of wickets 9, 22, 42, 85, 113, 150, 160, 230, 235

5, 33, 39, 131, 132, 210, 298, 333

Bowling *First Innings* Gough 21-7-52-3; Headley 27.3-4-72-4; Caddick 14-2-52-1; Ealham 11-2-34-2; Croft 4-0-13-0 *Second Innings* Gough 20-3-62-0; Headley 29-4-104-4; Croft 39-12-105-2; Ealham 13-3-41-1; Caddick 21-0-69-1

England

M A Butcher st Healy b Bevan	51	c McGrath b Gillespie	28
*M A Atherton c Healy b McGrath	5	lbw b Gillespie	21
†A J Stewart c Taylor b Warne	30	b Warne	1
N Hussain c Healy b Warne	13	lbw b Gillespie	1
G P Thorpe c Taylor b Warne	3	c Healy b Warne	7
J P Crawley c Healy b Warne	4	hit wkt b McGrath	83
M A Ealham not out	24	c Healy b McGrath	9
R D B Croft c S R Waugh b McGrath	7	c Reiffel b McGrath	7
D Gough lbw b Warne	1	b McGrath	6
A R Caddick c M E Waugh b Warne	15	c Gillespie b Warne	17
D W Headley b McGrath	0	not out	0
Extras (b 4, lb 3, nb 2)	9	(b 14, lb 4, w 1, nb 1)	20
Total (84.4 overs)	162	(73.4 overs)	200

Fall of wickets 8, 74, 94, 101, 110, 111, 122, 123, 161

44, 45, 50, 55, 84, 158, 170, 177, 188

Bowling *First Innings* McGrath 23.4-9-40-3; Reiffel 9-3-14-0; Warne 30-14-48-6; Gillespie 14-3-39-0; Bevan 8-3-14-1 *Second Innings* McGrath 21-4-46-4; Gillespie 12-4-31-3; Reiffel 2-0-8-0; Warne 30.4-8-63-3; Bevan 8-2-34-0

Australia won by 268 runs
Umpires G Sharp and S Venkataraghavan
Toss Australia

Splits

		Lunch	Tea	Close
First day	Australia	78-3	162-7	224-7
Second day	Australia	235		
	England	37-1	110-4	161-8
Third day	England	162		
	Australia	78-3	154-5	262-6
Fourth day	Australia	367-8	395-8 dec	
	England		49-2	130-5
Fifth day	England	200		

I

First Day

On this Thursday morning in Manchester two questions hover over the beginning of the Test. The first is, will Old Trafford give us something of decisive significance for the series, a 2-0 lead for England, a levelling of things for Australia? Four years ago Australia got off to a flying start on this ground in the first Test and never looked back; eight years ago they regained the Ashes here. The morning press is thick with comment about Old Trafford, watersheds and the like. Frank Keating compares the situation in the present series to 30-15 at tennis: if you go ahead 40-15, it gives you a cushion against error or bad luck; if you level it to 30-30, the momentum can carry you through to victory.

The second question is, inevitably, the weather. For some days the forecast has been gloomy, with no real prospect of a break toward sunshine until Saturday. After Lord's this is worrying. We don't look forward to having to hang about again. But when I wake it is dry, and I phone Ian to establish that we are definitely going to the ground for the beginning of play at 11.00. No question about it, he assures me. It's not raining where he is either.

However, Manchester having been for 30 years my home – and Old Trafford, consequently, my cricketing home – the venue of this Test introduces a new element into Ian's and my situation. He will be leaving for the ground from our common place of work, the Department of Government in the University of Manchester. Hardworking fellow that he is, Ian likes to knock off a few chores in the office before the start of play. It is convenient to meet him there – a friend, Vittorio, who is joining us for the first two days, will also do so – as he is the one with the car. But though I concede nothing to Ian in dedication to duty, on a Test match day it is not congenial to me to compromise this one-sixth segment of my summer holiday with work-related matters. At cricket I am with cricket: its rhythms, its ambience, the logic of each developing situation. This is, more or less wholly, where I want to be for the days of the game.

Still, there is the matter of the lift, and anyway I need to make sure that Ian doesn't get so diverted as to do something silly and leave for the ground too late or, worse still, decide to miss a morning. I have had a slight worry about him in this respect right from the start. Ian can get fidgety when hanging out or with not too much actively to occupy him. He is known to go into the office on a Sunday! Might the hectic demands of our profession lure him from the slow, drawn-out patience of spectating at cricket? Not really. After two Tests he is well and truly hooked. But I go into the Department all the same, and in order not to be tainted, from a cricketing point of view, by this association with work, I remind myself that the Department of Government also has its own august connections with the game. There is not quite as rich a heritage as at Lord's or Old Trafford, but we have had at least two well-known alumni in this area. The first is one of the greats, Frank Worrell, West Indian all-rounder and captain; with Clyde Walcott and Everton Weekes, part of 'the three Ws' of an earlier era. Worrell was a student in the Faculty in the 1950s. The second is Matthew Engel, brilliant journalist and present editor of *Wisden*. Only yesterday, remembering his long relationship with the ground, Engel wrote in the *Guardian* of how he revised for his finals at Old Trafford. I check to see if there is still paper-work on these two former students amongst our ageing files, and there is.

Thus protected by my researches from anything unduly intrusive upon thoughts of cricket, I set out with Ian and Vittorio, and we arrive at our seats in the MacLaren Stand to find that Taylor has won the toss for the third time in a row and elected to bat. I like this. We admire the new giant replay screen, of sharper definition, it seems to us, than those at Edgbaston and Lord's, and Ian and I disagree as to how Old Trafford compares with Edgbaston for general character and attractiveness. He thinks there's not much in it, though allowing that the pavilion here makes a small difference in Old Trafford's favour. Me, I love Old Trafford. I find it brighter and more compact, less down-at-heel, than Edgbaston. Perhaps the comparison is affected by the number of times I have been here. Never mind. Ian's opinion is soon compromised by the admission that his affection for the Birmingham ground is increased by the outcome of the Test there. What a lack of objectivity.

The first morning belongs to England. Thanks to some probing and accurate bowling, especially from Dean Headley who is making his Test debut in this match, Australia are soon up against the ropes. For the first 20 minutes there is much playing and missing, a drama every ball. The spectators around us are more keyed up and impressionable than those at Edgbaston or Lord's. There is an 'ooh' for each ball that passes the bat, an 'aah' for every miscue. Taylor is caught at slip by Thorpe off Headley, a hair's breadth from the turf, and gone cheaply again for 2; Blewett plays a ball from Gough on to his stumps, trying to attack too early in his innings perhaps; and Mark Waugh is caught by Stewart off Ealham. 42 for 3. I begin to rue Australia's winning of the toss. Throughout the morning there are spots of rain but the real stuff holds off. Australia make it through to lunch without further loss.

The middle session of the day starts 20 minutes late because of rain and contains a second, 35-minute stoppage. It too belongs to England. The procession of Australian batsmen continues, not a rush as at Edgbaston, but a steady flow, with modest partnerships between the fall of wickets. Headley, continuing a fine display of testing bowling, claims the next two, Elliott caught by Stewart for 40, and Bevan likewise for 7. Bevan's place must now surely be in question. He has done nothing yet in this series with the bat and his bowling at Lord's was erratic, to put it mildly. Headley's debut has been impressive. He is the grandson of the legendary George Headley – known as the 'black Bradman' and one of those few Test cricketers with a batting average above 60 – and the son of the lesser Ron who played two Tests for the West Indies in 1973. It is the first time three generations of a family have played at Test level. Dean looks every inch the part. After the interruption for rain, Stewart bags two more catches to make it five to this point in the innings: Healy off Caddick and Warne off Ealham, both for insignificant scores. Australia go to tea on 162 for 7. I am beginning really to worry about their hold on the Ashes, as I confess to Ian and Vittorio.

And yet, cricket rarely letting one's perceptions settle for too long in the same place, the last session brings some light into the darkness. Darkness: the longest interruption of play without any actual rain I personally can remember witnessing, nearly an hour and a half simply on account of the light not being good enough. I would discover on returning home that not far away the same cloud mass blackening the sky at Old Trafford was dumping its rain on Withington and Didsbury. We were therefore lucky. Play was able to restart at 6.10, as it could not have done had we had the downpour instead of the darkness.

Light: the batting of Steve Waugh. In the final 14 overs Reiffel is dropped by Stewart off Headley, Croft has an appeal for a catch from the same batsman turned down – the catcher once again Stewart who is at the heart of things today, and the decision, it appears, wrong – and Waugh and Reiffel post the first fifty partnership of the innings. Just before close of play, in Stygian gloom, Waugh cuts Croft fiercely to the boundary to reach his hundred. It is his thirteenth in Tests. We have been watching from much earlier to see if he can hoist his average back above 50. It has dipped just under that since the beginning of the series, and he was needing 85 to restore it. His century now serves Australia well, turning their innings into something at least reasonable – or so I would say, but more of this in a moment – where earlier it had looked as though it would be quite insufficient. The century is typically Steve Waugh: nothing showy, just concentration, doggedness and an old Australian kind of toughness, punctuated by a punishing severity towards anything overpitched or giving room outside off stump to drive or cut. Waugh is the business; in the context of today's play a champion. It is not for the first time. On his day he is a performer to admire and his days come relatively often. Ian has been worried enough by the partnership between him and Reiffel to jib at the non-begrudging rule agreed by us at Edgbaston: once he passes 94 an opposing batsman is to be 'hoped' towards his hundred, whereupon good riddance to him again. But Ian wants the partnership over. He applauds Waugh's hundred nevertheless. Play closes for the day on 224 for 7.

On the BBC highlights in the evening Geoff Boycott and Ian Chappell are both of the view that Australia have done not just reasonably on this wicket but well. Richie Benaud seems to lean in that direction too. I'm not so sure. Two hundred and some? I decide to do a bit of research before bed to refresh my memory on other Anglo-Australian games I have watched on this ground, and this is what I find. Two hundred and whatever in the first innings is quite regular here. In 1977 Greg Chappell's Australians made 297 and lost, in 1981 England made 231 and won, and 1985 was rain affected and drawn, but Australia made 257 on first innings. In 1989 England made 260 and went on to lose, and in 1993 Australia made 289 and won. A curiosity is that at the end of the first day in 1989, England were 224 for 7, the very same close of play score as today. To repeat, England went on to lose. Another day, a different game. Roll on 11.00am.

Second Day

The game tilted decisively Australia's way this afternoon and even though they failed to ram home their advantage in the final hour, they must be considered to retain a significant edge. The man mainly responsible was Shane Warne, who came into his own for the first time in the series, taking 5 wickets for 48; the same Shane Warne Ian thinks is over the hill, habitually referring to him as 'the trundler'. Mind you, Ian has been affecting this attitude since not long after Warne dismissed Gatting here in 1993 with that unforgettable opening delivery, so he may not be completely serious. In any event, he became somewhat ruminative during England's decline. The weather left us alone. Despite the forecasts we had no interruptions for rain for the first time since the Thursday at Edgbaston. In a day full of action and incident there were some sharply etched moments.

Piwi was with us. Leaving Hitchin at some unholy hour of the morning he was outside my door by 8.00 while I was still writing up my account of yesterday's play. So that I could finish and he be fully primed when the second day began, Adèle settled him in front of the highlights which we had recorded the night before. We then drove to the ground at a normal sort of time, arriving shortly after 10.00, and took our seats in D North, very nicely positioned behind the slips. Ian – it's probably not worth continuing to report this even – just scraped in 10 minutes before play began, bringing with him Vittorio who appeared not to realise how late they were.

England wrapped up the Australian innings in just over half an hour. Gough bowled Reiffel and Waugh, and Stewart took his sixth catch of the innings to dismiss Gillespie off the bowling of Headley. Headley had missed a sharp return catch from Gillespie the ball before. He finished with four well-deserved wickets. Gough's two dismissals were beauties, both deliveries pitched in the block hole, the first taking out Reiffel's off stump, the second played on by Waugh to pad and then wicket. The one which yorked Reiffel is the first moment standing out for me from this day's play. It was on the spot and Reiffel had not so much as a whiff of it as it went by to remove his off stump as clean as can be.

So Australia 235. I comb through the precedents again in my mind: 1977 and 1981, 1989, 1993. What sort of 200-plus will this turn out to be? Ian, as well as recording the usual side bets between him and me, is busy arranging more extended wagers between the four of us.

Atherton and Butcher begin watchfully, the runs coming slowly at just one per over. But Atherton is soon out with the score on 8, gloving a ball from McGrath down the leg-side to Healy. It is more careless than one expects from him. Warne fails to seize a brilliant run-out opportunity just before lunch, his throw missing the stumps at his, the bowler's, end with Stewart well out of his ground. England go to lunch on 37 for 1. Our friend Paul, also from the Department, comes over to say hello and we chat about the prospects. Then after lunch Butcher and Stewart take their partnership past 50. England seem to be building towards a decent innings total – as I expect, my side bet with Ian having fixed on 327, following the models of 1977 and 1989 when the team batting second achieved a substantial lead. It is what Ian expects too, his bet on England's total being 315. However, things now start to happen. First Stewart is taken by Taylor, diving at slip, off the bowling of Warne. He has made 30 and England are 74 for 2. Then Butcher is stumped by Healy off Bevan for 51 and it is 94 for 3. Butcher's has been a solid, patient half-century.

Healy's stumping is the real moment of the day for me. It is one of those occasions in cricket when time stops for an instant as... *something happens.* CLR James has a striking description of the experience. Everyone feels it, the drama of the event, though some are not altogether sure just *what* has happened. There is a buzz as it is clarified – and it is over. And we have been there, together, in the strangeness of the moment. In the present case Butcher, who had been looking well in, missed a ball from Bevan and in the follow through from the attempted shot, moved just inches out of his crease. Healy had the bails off in a flash and was running down the pitch to embrace Bevan in celebration, though no one else – not the square-leg umpire, not the batsman himself nor anyone in the crowd – was sure if Butcher was even out or not. The third umpire and TV replay were called upon to assist, but Healy *knew.* And I therefore did also, sensing that Healy's reaction was genuine joy, not the choreographed appeal which all teams now engage in when they think they might get the umpire's decision. The stumping itself, technically, was the most beautiful piece of wicket-keeping you could see and appropriately it was Healy's hundredth dismissal in Ashes cricket. But the whole experience of the moment is one that will stay in my mind forever.

A collapse now ensued on either side of tea. Thorpe was caught at slip by Taylor off Warne. The batsman stood his ground, whether insolently or only reluctantly, but the TV replay offered no support for his delaying. Hussain and Crawley were both caught by Healy, also off Warne, who went on to trap Gough lbw. The guy was weaving his spell again at last: tying the batsman down, worrying him, turning the ball out of the rough created by the bowler's footmarks and with all the vocal and facial accompaniment that is part of his performance. 'Warne's old magic leaves England mesmerised' as the *Guardian* headline of the following morning had it, and this was the truth. The trundler had trundled another beauty. He is the leg-spinner supreme, a giant not of those days but of these.

In there amongst Warne's dismissals was one more for McGrath, and this was another memorable moment of my day. Steve Waugh took a lovely catch running and diving to his right at mid-off. Not that there have not been tougher catches, but this one was particularly pleasing to the eye. After all that, at 123 for 8, England looked well and truly up the creek without a paddle, Ian seemed worried and I was hoping for an excellent, hundred-plus lead and, simultaneously, beginning to fret that Australia might have a short, uncomfortable session to bat through at the end of the afternoon. But as is the way of things in cricket, England now rediscovered the paddle at least. Caddick and Ealham negotiated the rest of the day, putting on 38, for England to close on 161. Warne and the other Australian bowlers could not part them. Caddick at one point padded up to a big leg-break from Warne and the ball found its way between his legs and nearly on to the stumps. He survived. Australia clearly have the advantage, but anything could still happen.

Third Day

Another day uninterrupted by rain, a day of proper summer during which the balance swung back and forth before Australia established what looks to be a commanding position. Nobody now is giving England much of a chance, except for me in my more pessimistic moments. Already they would need 336 to win the match and they have still to capture the last four Australian wickets. It doesn't look good for them. But, you know, fat lady and the rest – it ain't over yet.

The stout resistance shown by England's ninth wicket partnership had vanished away in the night, and Caddick was caught by Mark Waugh (at the third attempt) in Warne's first over, giving the trundler a final tally of 6 for 48. McGrath then disposed of Headley in the manner Gough had disposed of Reiffel on the previous morning, with a ball cleanly taking out off stump, and the innings was ended for the addition of only one run. Advantage Australia.

The Australian innings began, with the lead 73, and we settled in (now back in the MacLaren Stand, Ian, Piwi and me) for what we knew must be a tense period of cricket, the destiny of this match and the shape of the whole series really on the line. Tense is what it was, speaking for myself anyway. It began with a small collapse. Taylor, Blewett and Elliott were all gone with the score only 39, Taylor and Elliott both caught at slip by Butcher off Headley, Taylor yet again for next to nothing. Headley was seeing off the left-handers as he had in the first innings. Blewett's dismissal, however, between these other two, was something else. He was 'caught' at slip by Hussain off Croft, from a ball that hit the ground before being scooped, fumbled and then latched on to again, with the fielder and England around him jubilant. The umpire, Venkat, had to confer with his colleague at square leg as Blewett stood his ground disbelievingly, but the decision went against him. Even on the replay screen and from the other side of the ground, this decision looked dubious, and later inspection of the incident on TV made it clear it was not a catch. It is the way of things these days for teams to go up for more or less anything they think they can get from the umpires, but that doesn't yet generally extend to appealing for a catch when the ball has hit the ground. The claim of this one by Hussain left a nasty taste. It puts in perspective Healy's contrasting conduct at Lord's and Selvey's cynical response to it in suggesting that Healy might merely have been worried what the cameras would reveal. Advantage, in any case, England.

The brothers Waugh were now together and on either side of lunch they compiled a partnership of 92. In the situation these were vital runs. The Waughs restored the Australian innings to normality, steadily building up the lead. During all the time they were together, it was heart-in-mouth concentration for the partisan spectator. Indeed, though this was a Saturday crowd, a full house that would normally have been very boisterous, until lunch and through the middle session of the day it was rapt, as though conscious of how much was at stake. Mark Waugh brought up his first half-century of the series with successive boundaries off Caddick, one of these a six over the mid-wicket rope. Steve battled along a little way behind him and it became more evident with each shot he played that the discomfort in his right hand – something I'd noticed initially towards the end of his first innings – was becoming more troubling. Yet the partnership continued to prosper. Advantage again Australia.

Then, as the tension was beginning to ease, Mark Waugh was bowled unexpectedly by Ealham, to be followed back to the pavilion in short order by Bevan, the latter once again proving vulnerable to the sharply rising ball. He was out caught off Headley for 0. Bevan must surely be dropped from the Australian side now. At 132 for 5, things once again had been rebalanced, and only at this point, in the last 10 minutes before tea, did the more senselessly determined of the spectators manage to get up the momentum to carry enough of the rest of the crowd into some circuits of the Mexican wave. Tea itself put an end to that. There was a certain amount of raucousness after tea also, but it wasn't too bad for a Test match Saturday. I toyed, optimistically, with the notion that a largely perceptive audience was influenced here by the crucial nature of the day's play in the context of the developing series.

On the way back to my seat at the end of the tea interval, I came across Patrick Eagar. Eagar's photographs during the 1980s formed the basis of books about the Tests of several summers to which Alan Ross supplied the commentary. These were all marvellous records of cricket, and since the sequence ended I have felt their absence. I asked Eagar if he was planning a book on the current series. He said probably not – 'unless England were unexpectedly to win it'. A pessimist of the opposing camp, evidently.

After tea Ian Healy continued where he and Steve Waugh had left off before it, putting together another valuable partnership, this one of 78. While Waugh stuck in there, protecting his painful hand, Healy hit out boldly, until, on 47, he lifted a catch to Butcher at mid-wicket off the bowling of Croft. I thought it a rash shot and said so to Ian and Piwi (though with some hyperbole, I'll grant). They shook their heads at me, in Ian's case with menaces about what he would say in his account of the day. On the evening's highlights, however, Richie Benaud, as ever incomparably wise, agreed with me. Warne now joined Waugh and in another half-century partnership they took Australia past the 300 lead. Warne laid about him and even hoisted a six off Headley, the pick of the England bowlers in this match. He

Nasser Hussain, scorer of a double century at Edgbaston
and a century at Headingley

LORD'S
Glenn McGrath celebrates the dismissal of John Crawley (top)
End of the England first innings (above)

OLD TRAFFORD
Steve Waugh, scorer of a century in each innings, leaves the field with Shane Warne at the end of the third day (above)

'Warne's old magic...' (left)

HEADINGLEY
Matthew Elliott (above) on
his way to scoring 199

Jason Gillespie about to
take off after bowling
Graham Thorpe (left)

HEADINGLEY
Thorpe, caught Mark Waugh (via Ian Healy), bowled Gillespie (top)
Victorious Australia (above)

TRENT BRIDGE
Mark Taylor (right)
'who can bat a bit'

Healy catching Alec
Stewart off the bowling
of Warne (below)

THE OVAL
Glenn McGrath (right),
7 for 76, and Australia's
man of the series

Andrew Caddick (below),
3 for 76, and 5 for 42

THE OVAL
Phil Tufnell (left),
man of the match
with 11 for 93

Triumphant England
(below)

© ALL PHOTOGRAPHS BY TOM JENKINS

was given not out to an appeal for a catch off the bowling of Croft, and this may have been another bad decision. My very moral friend Piwi, noticing at this point that Stewart behaves visibly aggrieved – the memory of an earlier decision of the day apparently erased from his mind – speaks with some yearning of CLR James. He invokes the spirit of 'It isn't cricket'.

When play is over he and I drive home to my place and, after collecting his stuff, Piwi heads off back to Hitchin. I'm sorry to see him go. Since the days in my back yard in 5 Cawston Street, Bulawayo, where I bowled slow off-breaks to him on the bare earth in the hope of becoming as good a bowler as Hugh Tayfield, Piwi and I have had cricket of one sort or another always with, and between, us.

The odds against England winning must now be long. If I can take a bet in the morning on them doing so, I will, as an insurance against disappointment.

Fourth Day

Early today Steve Waugh notched up an achievement that hasn't been seen in Ashes cricket for 50 years, since the series of 1946-47 when, remarkably, both Denis Compton and Arthur Morris did it in the same match. He scored a century in both innings of the game. Heaven knows what he'll do if he gets to play another Test at Old Trafford. In 1989 here he made 6 and 64; in 1993, batting only once, he made 92; and in the present Test he has made 108 and 116. England can perhaps take some comfort that the gaps in this numerical sequence are getting smaller. If Australia are now in a position to level the series on the final day of the game, what they owe to Waugh in getting there is enormous. And unless England can mount one of the great rearguard actions of Test history, that is how things are now poised.

I took a taxi to the ground this morning with a driver who said he was a friend of Wasim Akram's. I bet a tenner with Ladbrokes, £5 each on an England win and the draw at 10 to 1 and 6 to 1 respectively. Rationally calculated, it is wasted money. But, seen differently, it comes into play, with Jenny's stone and some other things, to exert a curious influence on events.

The day began brilliantly for Australia. They rattled up 30 in the first three overs, Warne in particular doing the business, including knocking the bowling of Headley about. He was eventually out for 53, and Reiffel joined Waugh who now remained perched for a few overs on 97, in sight of his historic achievement. He played some tight, nagging bowling from Croft with extreme concentration and care. When at last he got there, the crowd rose to him in recognition of his rare feat. It had been a courageous effort. Waugh departed and we reckoned the Australian innings must soon be over, but Gillespie and Reiffel then added another substantial partnership, this one of 62, to follow the 88 and 35 that had preceded it. Incredibly in the light of earlier happenings in this game, Australia were in sight of 400 when Taylor declared 20 minutes after lunch with two wickets standing. He had left England to score 469 to win – were they to make it, a record winning total for a Test match.

Atherton and Butcher put together a sound start, and as their partnership reached the 40s I began to worry slightly. I know the history, the long odds and all the rest of it. Even so, just three runs an over, a goodish batting side and more than a day and a half to go. Somebody, some time, has to rewrite the record book. Not, however, today. 44 for 1, 45 for 2, 50 for 3, 55 for 4, 84 for 5 – and this particular fear was soon laid to rest. By the time Crawley, with the help of Mark Ealham, staged some resistance late in the day with a plucky half-century, the best of England's top order was gone. First Atherton lbw to Gillespie, then Stewart beautifully bowled by Warne, then Hussain the same way as Atherton and to the same bowler. Ian on my left appeared perceptibly to start with each of these dismissals. I knew how he felt from my experience at Edgbaston. My suggestion that it was good for our journal of the series if things were now evened up didn't convince him, and frankly I have myself scorned such arguments in the past when England supporters have said to me it would be 'good for the series' if Australia, ahead at the time, were to lose one. Yet it is true, also, that before the series began, when the partisan emotions were not yet fully aroused, we had agreed that we were as keen on there being a good contest as we were on the result. In any event when McGrath, running in at long leg, took an outstanding catch from Butcher – hooking – to give Gillespie his third wicket of the day, I was elated. 'These guys,' says Ian, 'are on a roll' and so they were. Warne then chipped in with a second wicket, getting Thorpe to nick one to Healy, before Crawley and Ealham managed to shut Australia out for the rest of the afternoon. Crawley had the assistance of some awful rubbish from

Michael Bevan, with whom Taylor persisted, one can only assume, for the few good deliveries mixed in with it.

The last part of the day was marred for me, in a minor way, by a ceaselessly talkative bloke with a dull, pedantic wit, sitting just behind us. It was marred more seriously by the antics of the know-nothings in the crowd. It seems that each time I dare to comment on their relative moderation one day, we are punished on the next by an unbearable cacophony. Today, apart from more than half a dozen streakers running on to the field to disrupt the play – and dealt with, it should be said, more effectively here at Old Trafford than elsewhere, each one quickly and expertly tackled to the ground by what look to be rugby-playing stewards – we had almost unending noise, abusive singing, a bowler retiring towards the boundary booed by the crowd behind him. My friend Morris who will be with us for the first day at Headingley (the Mecca of this kind of stuff), calls it 'the English disease'. Not having watched cricket anywhere else than England lately, I don't know if he is right about this. It is proper, anyway, to record it here. In an account aiming to relate how two cricket-loving spectators experienced the Ashes series of 1997, it would not be either accurate or honest to pass over the fact that the enduring beauty of Test cricket is today mired within something uglier. Those who encourage it – David Hopps in the *Guardian* on the eve of the Lord's Test, and the England captain, Michael Atherton, himself – do not know fully of what they speak. Neither of them is obliged to sit at cricket in a sea of baying supporters and endlessly cavorting louts. To reverse the trend may not be easy but something does need to be done about it. In the circumstances of today, I personally give some consideration to the use of keel-hauling.

England are 130 for 5. Could they, in spite of everything, hold out?

Fifth Day

I cycled to Old Trafford this morning. Nearing Chorlton I passed another cyclist, an older man, rucksack on back, and asked him if he might be on his way to the ground too. I wanted to know where I could safely leave my bike. He knew the answer but wasn't going. 'Too dismal a prospect,' he said. 'I'm going to the dentist. Much more inviting.'

In the end, the best precedent for the general shape and outcome of this game was the last time England and Australia fought it out here, 1993. As on that occasion, Australia made a first innings total that seemed to me not quite enough in the conditions but came away nonetheless with a first innings lead of 70-odd. As then also, the third innings of the match was the biggest, leaving England with a monumental task. In 1993 Australia went on to win by 179 runs; today they won by 268. The major difference is that last time England put up a stronger resistance, the game only concluding late on the final afternoon. In 1989 too – albeit in a different situation since Australia could still bat again if need be and indeed they had to – Russell and Emburey held them up through the last morning and into the afternoon before the breakthrough came. Today England folded in an hour and a half. The game was over before lunch.

The man who did the damage was not, as generally expected, Shane Warne, but (my bowler in the side bets) Glenn McGrath. He had Ealham caught by Healy and Croft caught at backward short leg off a rising delivery, and then bowled Gough off stump, all three of them for single-figure scores. In the one remarkable dismissal of the morning, Crawley, the only batsman in this innings significantly to slow the Australian surge towards victory, went too far back in playing a shot off McGrath out towards point and he stepped on his wicket. This was the more remarkable in that it was the second dismissal hit wicket in consecutive Tests, Atherton going the same way at Lord's. Warne then had Caddick caught by Gillespie and the series was levelled.

Ian seemed more relaxed this morning than earlier in the England innings, resigned by now to the inevitable, I guess. But was he really so relaxed? There were outer signs of a moral collapse as, at 12.20, he announced he was eating his lunch – a succumbing to weakness the two of us had fought against all series, even when feeling hungry by mid-morning. I decided to follow suit and eat mine as well, so disguising from Ian the underlying significance of his behaviour. He took the defeat graciously, congratulating me for Australia's performance, as if by my secret ploys I had contributed to it. I thanked him and headed off towards the pavilion to see the closing ceremonies.

We watched cricket in peace today and as it used to be. Old Trafford was perhaps a quarter to a third full and the 'Ingerland' contingent were thin on the ground. Spectators applauded the end of an over and anything creditable by an opposition player. Or maybe it would be more true to say that they did this and it could be heard. We could even make out some of what the woman a couple of rows down from us (Mark Taylor's wife as it turned out) was saying to her interviewer. Only in front of the pavilion at the end did the 'Ingerlish' re-emerge, achieving a sufficient concentration there to start up a chant of 'You fat bastard' at Shane Warne. No one conducting the ceremony on the pavilion balcony above so much as invited them to moderate their behaviour.

The hell with them. Today Australia won a fine victory. Steve Waugh was chosen as man of the match. The Australian supporters in front of the pavilion offered a few gentle choruses of 'Aussie, Aussie, Aussie, oi, oi, oi', which I thought about giving a more Jewish inflection ('oy, oy, ooyy...') to register some of the anxiety I had suffered just getting to this point in the series. They forbore from singing 'Ashes staying put' – in reply to the 'Ashes coming home' which we had had to endure from Edgbaston onwards – and a good thing too. The series is wide open, English doom and gloom on the heels of an undue euphoria notwithstanding. Hostilities resume in Leeds in just over a fortnight.

I make my way back to the stands and I wait there and wonder. I wonder for the hundredth time why it matters, the winning of your team. Today I am really happy because 11 men have won a game. I remember other winning last days at Old Trafford: Australia in 1989 and 1993; the West Indians in 1984 and 1988; and *England* in 1995, who – yes – I was supporting then against the West Indies, and *what* support, it induced a hat-trick from Dominic Cork on the fourth morning and victory with a day to spare. I remember also the very first such occasion of my life, at the Wanderers in Johannesburg in 1957 after the Springboks had beaten Peter May's team in the fourth Test of the series, Hugh Tayfield taking nine wickets in the second innings and 13 altogether in the match. I remember the drive back to Bulawayo from Johannesburg later, 500 miles through the night, and that distinctive inner feeling (stronger at the age of 13) as I slept in the back of the car, relishing the victory and Tayfield's part in it. I generally linger like this at Old Trafford at the end of a Test match, reluctant to draw a line under it all, reluctant to leave. I wonder now about my hypothesis, after Lord's, of the declining and the rising curves: England and Australia, Ian and me. At this point £1.50 down, I seem to have been wrong about the side bets but right about the cricket. I am willing to settle for that share-out. So long as the cricket curve continues up, the side bet curve can continue down.

I cycle back to the Department of Government at the University of Manchester, one-time place of Frank Worrell and of the future editor of *Wisden*. And the place of my professional life and duties for three decades now and of Ian's for not so long as that. Ian is back there before me. I already have an e-mail from him.

II

Thursday

Things soon change. The Ashes series which only two weeks previously had loomed large in the nation's preoccupations was by the start of the Old Trafford Test of little more than peripheral interest. Partly this was because England's bubble had been burst in the first innings at Lord's. Chiefly it was because unusually good British tennis performances at Wimbledon had captured the nation's attention and pushed cricket out of the media spotlight. On the first day of the third Test Britain had two players competing in the men's quarter-finals for the first time since 1961: Tim Henman against Michael Stich (the 1991 champion) and Greg Rusedski against Cedric Pioline. Small wonder, then, that the Ashes series was no longer the main story.

The period since the Lord's Test had also witnessed further developments in the sporting fortunes of Norm and me. Out of the blue on the Friday between Tests Manchester United had announced to the world, and Norm by phone had reported to me, the £3.5 million purchase of Spurs' best player and England international, Teddy Sheringham, as a replacement for Cantona. More glee for Norm, more misery for me. The key factor in Sheringham's decision was said to be his failure to win a single domestic honour with Spurs (or any other team), and his belief that his best chance of doing so was with United. It was Norm's very point.

The one thing that had not changed between Tests was the weather, which remained wet, cold and thoroughly unpleasant throughout. I lost track of precisely how bad June's weather was, but it was certainly the wettest for more than a century. And now the Ashes series was moving to Manchester of all places! Was another rain-affected draw in prospect? For several days prior to the Test Norm and I sought forecasts from people encountered in the office, at the bridge club, even on the street, but none gave us comfort. Thursday and Friday would definitely be bad. Come Saturday? Projections differed, but it seemed that there was some possibility of sunshine. We prepared ourselves to lose significant amounts of play in this match.

It was therefore something of a surprise – and certainly a pleasant one – when the first day dawned dry, though also overcast. As Norm and I made our way to the ground with our buddy Vittorio, who was joining us for the first two days, we figured that at the very least we would get play at 11.00. Not bad going. Benefiting from Norm's Lancashire CCC membership, we took our seats in the MacLaren Stand of the members' enclosure. Once again they were good: not quite up to the standard set at Lord's, but still with a fine view down the wicket from the Stretford End. Although we were not particularly early – 10.50 when we reached our seats – we still had time to take in the surroundings, place side bets, and work out how Vittorio could be allowed a punt or two without disrupting the serious business taking place between Norm and me. About the ground, Norm and Vittorio said all sorts of nice things while I begged to differ. Certainly Old Trafford has a much nicer pavilion than Edgbaston, but it looks side on which is plain daft. I also find Old Trafford a very flat ground, and see little merit in the small number of buildings and stands that relieve the monotony.

Australia had again won the toss – three in three so far – and reverted to Edgbaston practice by opting to bat. Had Taylor been reading up on Old Trafford history? No side, it turns out, has ever won a Manchester Test by putting the opposition in. In the overcast conditions in which the match was starting it certainly seemed a bold decision. The two teams were largely unchanged, Australia bringing the in-form Gillespie back in place of Kasprowicz, England giving a first cap to Kent's Dean Headley in place of Devon Malcolm. Headley, all the papers noted, was both son and grandson to Test cricketers – Ron and George – who played for the West Indies: a unique instance of three generations of the same family playing cricket at Test level. Malcolm, Christopher Martin-Jenkins noted in the *Daily Telegraph*, had been given only seven overs by Atherton at

Lord's. Norm and I naturally computed all this information in making our side bets. Norm: Mark Waugh (as ever), Croft, 327. Ian: Blewett, Caddick, 196. On a side bet to incorporate Vittorio, we opted for wickets down in the first session. Vittorio: 1. Norm: 2. Ian: 4. The two losers each to give the winner 50p.

Norm and I also talked about previous trips to the ground. 1992 had featured the now legendary (among us) day when we came in a group of seven or eight to see England play Pakistan and all placed side bets on the number of runs David Gower would make. By lunch he had reached 69 (in the process passing Geoffrey Boycott's record 8114 runs in Tests for England), and only Norm and I were still in the frame with 73 and something like 118 respectively. Sure enough, Gower after lunch fluked a boundary through the slips and was then dismissed for the very 73 Norm had selected. 1993 had seen Mike Gatting bowled in the first innings by Shane Warne with the 'ball from hell', Warne's first in Ashes cricket, and in the second by Merv Hughes with the final delivery of the fourth day. Although on the fifth day Graham Gooch went on to make a century before being out handled ball, Australia took England's last wicket inside the final hour to win the match. At the time Norm held Gatting's fourth-day dismissal to be 'crucial' in preventing an England victory, even though the target they had been set was something enormous in the 500 range. One of those years, or possibly 1995 when the West Indies came, stayed in the memory not just because of the cricket but also because in K Stand next to the MacLaren Stand where we were sitting both Gary Lineker and Cecil Parkinson had been spotted. Or did they come to two different matches?

There was no time to ponder the question: the morning session was about to start and our attention turned to that. To my great satisfaction events quickly settled into an Edgbastonian pattern. Taylor went cheaply – of course – caught Thorpe (low down at first slip), bowled Headley for 2. Australia 9 for 1 and a prize first scalp in Test cricket for Headley. My man Blewett followed, chancing his arm rather too early in the innings and dragging a ball from Gough on to his stumps. 22 for 2. In many ways, however, the Australians got off lightly in the opening skirmishes, for England's opening pair of Gough and Headley bowled beautifully, came within a whisker of finding the outside edge on numerous occasions, and generally looked like one of the most dangerous attacks England have fielded in years. Gough, leading off, was his usual bounce, fire and 110 per cent effort. Headley, almost sleek and smooth enough to be in the 'whispering death' mould of Michael Holding, made an immensely impressive debut, bowling a line and length which were consistently excellent. The two of them also rattled through their overs: 15 in the first hour. It helped that the batsmen rarely got the ball off the square or even laid a bat on it at all: Australia managed 26 for 2 from those 15 overs. But the occasional traffic to and from the pavilion slowed things down and still England's opening bowlers maintained a purposeful rhythm.

In the next hour the Australians picked things up a little. In a further 15 overs they took their score to 78 for 3, losing only Mark Waugh – caught Stewart, bowled Ealham – for 12. 78 for 3 struck me as pretty fair going for both sides: the wicket was by no means easy and 250 would surely be a good total. Norm was not convinced: 70-30 in England's favour according to him. He also said that he now seriously believed England would win the series. On less important matters we noted that none of us had won the wickets-down side bet, pondered the significance of stirrings from the Barmy Army even before lunch on the first day, and bemoaned the lack of a single decent celebrity in K Stand (though later Geoff Marsh, the Australian coach, did show up).

Still, for Norm and me it was good simply to make it to lunch without succumbing to the temptation of a bite to eat. As the series progressed we seemed to be getting hungry earlier and earlier. Norm at 11.50 here at Old Trafford: 'Hm, I feel a bit peckish now'. But it could just as easily have been me. Norm drew the parallel with rail travel. You board a train in Manchester and find it impossible to get even as far as Macclesfield without tucking into your sandwich. At the cricket we were still managing to hold out till 1.00, but the exercise of will was becoming massive.

As we ate some spots of rain fell, but that had also happened during the morning session and play had not been disrupted. After lunch, however, the umpires chose to keep the players in the pavilion until 2.00 before allowing the match to resume. The paying public, though grumpy, kept its discontent largely to itself. A feeble – and vain – attempt was made to institute a Mexican wave. The three of us placed a complex series of side bets on runs scored during the session. Norm: 74-83. Ian: 87-96. Vittorio: 67-73 and 84-6. In the short passage of play that then followed, Australia progressed to 126 for 5 at a run a minute. Elliott, who had played and missed all day, went finally for 40. Bevan, who had played and missed all series, went quickly enough for 7. Both were caught by Stewart off Headley, who was still bowling superbly. Rain then generated a 35-minute interruption. The umpires prompted more public discontent by inspecting a perfectly dry and playable pitch at 3.10 and setting the resumption for 3.25. Even in the abbreviated afternoon session which was therefore possible before a late tea at 4.10 the Australians looked like exceeding all of our side bets. Only a slowing up immediately before the interval halted them on 162 for 7 and handed the cash to Vittorio.

In the final session it was not rain that was the problem but bad light. Only 15 minutes' play were possible before three lights appeared on the scoreboard and the Australian batsmen – Steve Waugh and Paul Reiffel – chose to go off with the score 173 for 7. Soon those lights became four and five. I guess about half of the morning's full house sat things out, patiently watching the skies for signs of better light, the tennis on the big screen from Wimbledon for evidence of British success (there was none: both Henman and Rusedski lost), and the lights on the scoreboard for traces of movement. Here we got lucky. Slowly the number fell from five to four to three and then – to much cheering – to two. At this point the umpires were persuaded to come out and inspect the scene, but for reasons no one could fathom they decided not to allow a resumption. Appropriately, the public reaction was hostile. 'It's bloody nonsensical that!' expostulated a red-faced Victor Meldrew type behind us. He was right. In case the message hadn't sunk in he repeated or rephrased it several times in the next few minutes as the umpires continued to sit on the issue. Finally, after an interruption of well over an hour, it was announced that play would resume in five minutes. Why not immediately? But at least the players were finally coming back for possibly 14 overs.

Those overs witnessed more light changes – down to no lights at all and back up again to five – but the Australians were now on a roll and, amazingly, Steve Waugh was close to a century. How had he done that? At each stage in his innings he seemed to put on 10 or 20 runs when no one was looking, and here he was now in the 90s. We had cottoned on to what was happening a little earlier, and had spent some time going over his numbers. They were of course excellent, but an average of 50 and a bit at the start of the series was now below the mark. Norm calculated that he needed 85 if out to return to 50. Waugh certainly managed that. From the first ball of the final over, bowled by Croft, he struck a boundary which took him to three figures and the ground rose to salute an excellent century. There had undoubtedly been some playing and missing, but in these conditions that was par for the course. Indeed, in this context the century was very fine indeed. Waugh had also had good support. Although Reiffel was dropped by Stewart off Headley when 13 and survived what looked like a good appeal for a catch behind off Croft in the final over, he too made it to the close – on 26 – with the result that the Australians now looked pretty good on 224 for 7 from the day's 69 overs.

The match seemed well poised. For England Headley had made an assured and accomplished debut: 3 for 67 from 23 overs. He was clearly here to stay, and had possibly brought an end to Devon Malcolm's Test career. For Australia, Waugh's century was a major achievement. Moreover, the 250 which I still thought likely to be a good first innings total was now well within the Australians' grasp, and they had certainly seized a large helping of initiative in that final passage of play which saw 51 runs added without loss. From here the match – and with it the series? – could go either way.

Friday

I made my way to the ground with Vittorio. As we were within range of our seats by 10.35, we made a quick trip to Ladbrokes. The only enticing odds – 80 to 1 – were on Gough as top England scorer. I placed a bet of £1, reasoning that an England collapse could provide him with the perfect stage for an explosive innings. Odds on the match were England 9 to 4, Australia 5 to 4, the draw 7 to 4. The odds on a draw seemed notably ungenerous. The weather was now excellent and even forecast to stay that way: surely this match would come to a clear finish.

We went off to find Norm and, today, his friend Piwi and played out the pre-match ritual: Norm good-naturedly remonstrating with me (or us) about how impossibly fine I (or we) have cut it by showing up at 10.45 (or 10.50). Because Norm could not take three guests into the members' enclosure, the four of us were seated in D Stand North at the Warwick Road End. In many ways these were even better seats than those in the MacLaren Stand. They came closer to looking wicket to wicket, and were very near the playing area. In the period before start of play we discussed the state of the match. My view was that 250 would certainly be a good score for Australia in the conditions they had faced, but that in the improved weather conditions England should now be able to take a first-innings lead by scoring 300-plus. Norm reported that the pundits on the previous night's BBC highlights – Richie Benaud, Geoffrey Boycott and Ian Chappell – held Australia to be in a good position. He himself doubted this. We also placed side bets on runs scored during the morning session – Piwi 120-9, Norm 82-91, Ian 92-101, Vittorio 72-81 – and settled to follow that session. It was a lovely day for watching cricket: bright and sunny, but with occasional cloud cover to stop spectators from getting completely frazzled; warm, but not hot. This was in fact the first day since the opening day of the series that we got through three full sessions of play without interruption. It was the only day of the series that did not even look like being disrupted at any point. The local environment was also pretty good. There was no singing – at least not until the afternoon when the odd chant was raised – and not a single Mexican wave. Instead, there was just the good-natured buzz of a cricket crowd. Here it was actually a lot more buzzy than it had been on the previous day, but for me that was not a problem. In any case, what grounds could we have for complaint when we spent most of the day chatting about our many and varied lunacies?

On the field England made an excellent and highly efficient job of mopping up the Australian tail, taking three wickets for 11 runs in 8.3 overs to close the innings on 235. Gough started things by bowling Reiffel for 31 with a ball that headed towards leg and middle stump – which Reiffel had covered with his bat – before moving with the precision of a guided missile to hit off. It was a superb delivery to end a very troublesome eighth-wicket partnership of 70. Gough then induced Waugh to play on – to middle stump – for an excellent 108 which Waugh himself was reported in the morning's papers to rank alongside the double hundred scored in Jamaica two years previously. Headley, having dropped Gillespie off his own bowling, promptly had him caught by Stewart next ball for 0. Shades of Gough at Edgbaston. Also shades of Healy at Edgbaston, for this catch gave Stewart six dismissals in the innings. Again we mulled over whether this equalled the Ashes record. Norm thought Rod Marsh and Jack Russell had both clocked up seven dismissals in an innings. Yet in the next morning's *Independent* Derek Pringle stated that Stewart had matched an Ashes record set by Russell six years previously.

First side bets blood to me: 50p for Australian innings total. For the England first innings we both looked to an England lead. Ian: Atherton, Reiffel, 315. Norm: Thorpe, McGrath, 327. The innings in fact got off to a very slow start: 37 for 1 after 18 overs at lunch with Atherton out for 5 was the extent of it. That made for only 48 runs in the session, by far the lowest-scoring full session of the series to date (and well below our estimates: all side bets were off). But from England's point of view this seemed eminently sensible: carefully build a foundation and then blow the Australians away. It wasn't to be. Although our tea-time score bets were mostly tipped towards some high scoring – Norm 129 for 3, Ian 142 for 2, Vittorio 80 for 4, Piwi 150 for 1 – the session yielded 103 for 4. Honours shared by Norm and Vittorio. For the final session we bet on Hussain's score at close of play: Ian 37, Vittorio 40, Piwi 23, Norm 41. That issue was quickly resolved when Hussain failed to add to his tea-time score of 13, and Piwi pocketed the cash.

The England collapse was thus substantial. In the passage of play either side of tea England progressed from 74 for 1 to 123 for 8, with only Butcher's 51 and Stewart's 30 coming close to respectability. Crawley was even out when the score was 111, possibly the first batsman in the series to fall on a danger number. In the final hour Ealham (23 not out) and Caddick (15 not out) played well to see England to 161 for 8 by stumps. But it was very clearly Australia's day, dominated by two superb performances. One came from Shane Warne, who for the first time made a decisive intervention in the series, bowling beautifully from the Warwick Road End for 5 for 48 off 28 overs and 12 maidens by the close. Stewart and Thorpe were both caught by Taylor at slip. Hussain and Crawley were snapped up by Healy. Gough was trapped lbw. No English batsman looked other than bemused. The other great performance was a single moment of inspiration, when Healy stumped Butcher off Bevan in the merest fraction of a second that Butcher, having failed to connect with a leg-side full toss, was airborne and thus out of his crease. This was a stroke of genius on Healy's part and I was certainly glad to witness it. I would, however, have no clear picture of it had it not been replayed on the big TV screen at the ground, for only side on and in slow motion could the full extent of Healy's achievement be grasped. I was there, but on this occasion my mental record is little different from that of the armchair fan.

Satisfaction then for Norm by the close. Also for Piwi, an ostensibly impartial spectator who in fact leans towards Australia on the grounds that Atherton – ball-tamperer – is not to be supported. And Aussie sledging? Piwi seemed to think things had changed on that front since Border's day. Vittorio had no commitments either way. To me it felt like the beginning of the end.

Saturday

For day three it was just Norm, Piwi and me, so we were back in the MacLaren Stand. We traded stories from the very nice pieces in the papers about Warne's five wickets, which took him to 248 in Tests and equalled the record for a leg-spinner set by Benaud, and about the Healy stumping off Bevan, his one hundredth Ashes dismissal (a milestone only previously reached by Knott and Marsh). The best piece, by Henry Blofeld in the *Independent*, linked the two performances by placing Warne and Healy alongside Underwood and Knott as deadly in combination. Norm reported that Jen was vigorously polishing her lucky stone on a beach in Crete. This, moreover, was the original lucky stone lately found under the bed. Crazy family. We considered the day ahead, all thinking that the England tail would wag a good bit more. A total in excess of 200, nudging towards the Australians' 235, was our guess.

It didn't turn out that way. Caddick, staunch the evening before, succumbed in the first over, caught Mark Waugh, bowled Warne. Headley was bowled by McGrath soon thereafter. England 1 for 2 on the day, 162 all out overall. Warne 6 for 48. Australia therefore had a lead on first innings of 73. In a low-scoring match it looked decisive. Again I had won the side bet for innings total, though I had been more than 150 out. Again neither of us had succeeded with bets on individual performances. Norm and I moved to betting on the Australian second innings. Norm: Mark Waugh (who simply had to come good one day), Headley, 210. Ian: Blewett, Croft, 234. We also engaged in a bit more celeb spotting. They turned out to be almost as disappointing as on the first day: just Geoff Marsh (again), a character who looked remarkably like him (except that he had grown a very full moustache since Thursday), and Max from *Brookside*.

The Australian innings took a highly predictable course, though none of us did in fact predict it. Taylor out for 1, caught by Butcher at second slip off Headley in the second over of the innings. Bevan out for 0, caught by Atherton at point when Bevan himself was still looking in the direction of square leg. Everyone else into double figures, with Steve Waugh leading the offensive and standing on 82 not out by the close.

In the early stages of the innings there was some hope for England fans. Headley again bowled beautifully, and his early success could even go some way to re-opening the Mark Taylor question later in the series. Blewett could have been out in the same over as Taylor when an edge fell just short of first slip. When Blewett did go – for 19 – it was controversially to a Hussain catch off Croft which may or may not have carried. My sense from the big screen replay at the ground was that it did not: the trajectory didn't look right. Reports from *Test Match Special* listeners stated that opinion in the commentary box was divided. Still, this dismissal contributed to a situation in which the Australians were 39 for 3 with Taylor, Blewett and Elliott back in the pavilion. Then, however, Steve Waugh, batting with a severely bruised right hand, anchored a series of 50 partnerships – 92 with brother Mark (who made 55), 78 with Healy (47) and an unbroken 52 with Warne (33 not out) – to see Australia to 262 for 6 by the close. It was surely an impregnable position.

In the margins of all this we naturally chewed over other matters. Norm, for example, added a sub-clause to the cricketing law – Geras's law – we had been testing all series. The main clause states that when a fielder takes a bump ball first bounce at least one person in the ground will go up for a catch. From our observations Geras's law seemed to be valid in all conditions. Now the sub-clause: that when a fielder breaks the wicket and appeals for a run out at least one person in the ground will acclaim the 'dismissal' even if the batsman is easily in his ground. The sub-clause also seemed well founded. Norm's further attempt at legislation was less plausible. 'I feel that Headley should be disqualified from bowling. There must be a law applying to a cricketer whose father and grandfather played Test cricket... on the Saturday of a Test... Don't you think?' Neither Piwi nor I did. And when Headley was taken off soon thereafter: 'There *is* such a law!' Piwi and I groaned.

In the afternoon and evening sessions the pall of depression that descended on me seemed to prompt no corresponding euphoria in

Norm. Even as the Australian lead climbed past 200 and 250 he remained as anxious as ever. When Healy was out for 47, pulling a delivery from Croft into Butcher's hands at mid-wicket, Norm denounced an 'insane' decision on Healy's part. Further 'insanity' followed from Warne, most of it resulting in the ball travelling rapidly across the ground to the boundary rope. Piwi and I maintained that it made little difference now: the lead was already sufficient. Norm, however, was having none of it. 'Remember I said that at the end of the game!' I promised to record the words of the sage.

By the close, however, when Australia had reached their 262 for 6, even Norm had to confess to a certain satisfaction. And why not? Only one result was now possible.

Sunday

The Sunday papers confirmed this. Australia's lead of 335 was greater than England's highest-ever total to win an Ashes Test batting last: 332 for 7 at Melbourne 70 years ago. It was way in excess of the highest winning score in a fourth innings at Old Trafford: 145 for 7 by South Africa in 1955. Norm and I – on our own again by this stage – settled to watch the game in equally anxious moods. Only mine, of course, was justified.

Disappointingly, the fourth day did not conform to the pattern established by its two predecessors. Instead of wickets falling and the innings being wrapped up very quickly in the morning session, batsmen had the upper hand. England took the new ball, with Headley and Gough bowling in tandem, and saw 30 runs come off the first three overs of the day as Warne moved to a half-century in 65 balls and Waugh neared a second century of the match. Then, however, the England bowlers at least managed to impose a modicum of control on proceedings. In overs four to nine of the day, only six runs were scored. To the first ball of the tenth over – Caddick's first of the day – Warne was out. The partnership for the seventh wicket had nevertheless added 88.

All this was, however, sub-plot. The main story of the fourth morning was Steve Waugh's progress towards a second century in the match, a feat, Norm told me before play started, managed by an Australian in an Ashes Test only twice previously (the last occasion being 50 years ago). Most of the ground was now focused on this, and the tension built and built until finally Waugh was there. His was an outstanding achievement. It also gave the third Test an historic event to rank alongside those registered in the first two Tests: Hussain's double hundred and McGrath's eight wickets in an innings. In the series this was the seventh century, which seemed pretty good when the first innings of the first two Tests had seen entire teams dismissed for 118 and 77.

Australia, however, were not content with Waugh's personal triumph. They wanted victory too – no doubt more – and pursued it with some verve in a morning session that yielded 105 for 2 in 31 overs. Batsmen continued to make it easily into double figures and partnerships to extend beyond any reasonable projection: 35 between Waugh and Reiffel, before Waugh was out – caught Stewart bowled Headley – for 116; 34 between Reiffel and Gillespie by lunch.

The Australian lead by this stage was 440 and some 150 overs remained in the match. Would – indeed should – Taylor declare at this point? Norm, true as ever to the Allan Border school of cricket captaincy, thought they should not. Mainly this reflected his natural caution. As he said about the morning's run feast, 'If Australia can do this, why can't England? That's what worries me Ian.' Partly it reflected his appreciation of the psychology of the game, and the demoralisation that each succeeding Australian run caused for England. Mark Taylor clearly agreed: out trooped Reiffel and Gillespie after lunch to add a further 28 runs to the Australian total and their ninth-wicket partnership (taking it to 62), before Taylor finally brought the misery to a close by declaring just after 2.00 on 395 for 8. Another side bet triumph for me on innings total, but it was hard to savour. England now had 141 overs to score 469 runs to win. Ian: Atherton, Warne, 269. Norm: Hussain, McGrath, 300.

Atherton and Butcher actually set to the task very effectively. Following opening partnerships in this match of 9, 8 and 5, they saw England comfortably and quite speedily into double figures. On 44, however, Atherton was patently lbw to Gillespie for 21. Thereafter, the rot rapidly set in. 44 for 1 became 45 for 2, 50 for 3 and 55 for 4, with Stewart and Hussain falling for 1 and Butcher going for 28. The ball with which Warne bowled Stewart was a reasonably straight one that sneaked between bat and pad, but it was still a superb sight. It was also Warne's 250th Test wicket. The catch which McGrath took to remove Butcher – off the bowling of

Gillespie – was stunning, taken at full diving stretch as the fielder ran in from long leg. The Australians had their tails up, and the wicket was doing so much that Healy was wearing a helmet to keep to Warne, and conceding byes on a basis that was unusually regular for a keeper of his ability and standing.

Norm and I traded our usual banter as the England batsmen came and went. Ian: 'Come on Alec Stewart!' Norm: 'Stewart? He's history!' Sadly he was. Ian: 'Come on John Crawley!' Norm: 'Crawley? He's a spent force!' Well, maybe not. By the close Crawley – profiting from some gifts from Bevan but also dealing very effectively with Warne – was 53 not out and had put on an undefeated 46 with Ealham, who had stuck around for more than an hour for his 5 runs. England 130 for 5 by the close. Only 339 runs to go.

As on the Sunday at Edgbaston, the Barmy Army was in good voice for most of the day. 'Ingerland, Ingerland, Ingerland', 'Oh Lanky Lanky, Lanky Lanky Lanky Lanky Lankershire' and 'Stand up for the Ingerland' were the staples, interspersed with 'You ate all the pies' and any other humiliations the boys could come up with. Mexican waves made it round the ground before and after lunch, though at all other times they fizzled out. A conga bounced through H Stand at 3.00. More disruptive were the many 'streakers' – mostly, in fact, partially clad – who made it on to the playing area. There must have been close to a dozen in total. Although they were captured far more efficiently at Old Trafford than at Edgbaston, and escorted from the pitch by a pair of sinister-looking men in smart blazers, they still held up the game. We were certainly deprived of an extra over at the end of the day when two men ran on from the members' seats. Norm and I agreed that this cannot be allowed to continue, though we did not have a clear solution to the problem.

Still there were no decent celebs, though Norm – remarkably – managed to identify Henry Kissinger, Elton John, David Gower and Tom King in the seats adjacent to ours. All four seemed to have changed a fair bit since I had last seen them.

One more day to Australia.

Monday

The day of judgment had arrived. England had been found guilty – of incompetence in a number of departments – and now simply had to find out what they would go down for. 300 runs? 250? The people around me on the street talked jokingly of being present to witness the miracle, but no one was under any illusion about the task at hand. The feel of the ground as I walked in past B&Q was decidedly low-key: already the paraphernalia of corporate hospitality were being dismantled.

Indeed, the ground was not very full, but boy was it pleasant. Scarcely a sound could be heard beyond that generated by the cricket itself. There was conversation, of course. But there was also a great deal of concentration on the business at hand. And appreciation: every run – from singles squirted through the slips to fours driven through the covers – and every over – whether wicket-generating or otherwise – was applauded. This low-key atmosphere was actually very nice for watching cricket.

That said, Norm and I did encounter some distraction. Upgrading ourselves to K Stand, we couldn't help but notice that one small cricket-playing boy just two rows in front of us was receiving an inordinate amount of media attention. Indeed, before long an entire TV crew was circling him as carefully as if he were some exotic animal rarely captured on film. When a succession of men then came to shake his mother by the hand we began to suspect something was up. Those suspicions were confirmed when in the closing overs of the match a fully-fledged interview was conducted. We gleaned from listening in that this was Mark Taylor's wife and (as it turned out) two sons. That, then, was explicable. But what was the guy with the dictaphone a few seats along doing? Taping our punditry? It seemed unlikely.

On the field of play events followed their expected course, as Australia took 90 minutes to wrap up the England innings: from 130 for 5 to 200 all out are the bare facts of the matter. Warne and McGrath bowled unchanged, on the day taking 1 for 42 and 4 for 32 respectively. At one stage it looked as if McGrath would end with five-for by taking the final five wickets of the match, but then Warne finished things by having Caddick caught by Gillespie for 17.

Crawley and Ealham initially took up where they had left off the day before, looking entirely capable of dealing with Warne and McGrath. Indeed, Crawley played some fine shots off Warne. When, however, the partnership was broken some 35 minutes into the day by McGrath's dismissal of Ealham – brilliantly caught one-handed by Healy for 9 – the wickets started to fall with a certain regularity. Most unfortunate was Crawley who, like Atherton at Lord's, stepped on his wicket when in shouting distance of a century. Crawley went for 83 and even Australian supporters clearly felt some sympathy for him. The most interesting over was McGrath's seventh and the day's fourteenth: 2-2-2-1-1-W. The W was Croft meeting his match, caught by Reiffel at backward square leg.

England 200 all out meant an Australian victory by 268 runs: as emphatic as England's nine-wicket win at Edgbaston. Good for the series, as Norm said to me. I certainly hope so. At least by the end of the Old Trafford Test I had increased my lead in side bets to £1.50. And the weather had at last been put in its place: this match had mainly been played in excellent conditions. Where to now on all these fronts? I guess it depends on how the curves and cycles pan out. Where to also for the brave new world that England's victory at Edgbaston was held to herald, not just for the nation's cricket team or even sports teams in general, but for the nation itself under the Blair government? Is that euphoric honeymoon now over?

I walked from the ground, leaving Norm to savour his triumph with the many other Aussies present. On the way out I passed Henry Kissinger and noted that he now speaks with an Australian accent. So that's why he's taken to following the game.

Fourth Test
Headingley
24-28 July

Scorecard

England

M A Butcher c Blewett b Reiffel	24		c Healy b McGrath	19
*M A Atherton c Gillespie b McGrath	41		c Warne b McGrath	2
†A J Stewart c Blewett b Gillespie	7		b Reiffel	16
N Hussain c Taylor b McGrath	26		c Gillespie b Warne	105
D W Headley c S R Waugh b Gillespie	22	(8)	lbw b Reiffel	3
G P Thorpe b Gillespie	15	(5)	c M E Waugh b Gillespie	15
J P Crawley c Blewett b Gillespie	2	(6)	b Reiffel	72
M A Ealham not out	8	(7)	c M E Waugh b Reiffel	4
R D B Croft c Ponting b Gillespie	6		c Healy b Reiffel	5
D Gough b Gillespie	0		c M E Waugh b Gillespie	0
A M Smith b Gillespie	0		not out	4
Extras (b 4, lb 4, w 1, nb 12)	21		(b 6, lb 4, nb 13)	23
Total (59.4 overs)	172		(91.1 overs)	268

Fall of wickets 43, 58, 103, 138, 154, 154, 163, 172, 172

23, 28, 57, 89, 222, 252, 256, 263, 264

Bowling *First Innings* McGrath 22-5-67-2; Reiffel 20-4-41-1; Gillespie 13.4-1-37-7; Blewett 3-0-17-0; Warne 1-0-2-0 *Second Innings* McGrath 22-5-80-2; Reiffel 21.1-2-49-5; Gillespie 23-8-65-2; Warne 21-6-53-1; S R Waugh 4-1-11-0

Australia

*M A Taylor c Stewart b Gough	0
M T G Elliott b Gough	199
G S Blewett c Stewart b Gough	1
M E Waugh c & b Headley	8
S R Waugh c Crawley b Headley	4
R T Ponting c Ealham b Gough	127
†I A Healy b Ealham	31
S K Warne c Thorpe b Ealham	0
P R Reiffel not out	54
J N Gillespie b Gough	3
G D McGrath not out	20
Extras (b 9, lb 10, nb 35)	54
Total (for 9 dec, 123 overs)	501

Fall of wickets 0, 16, 43, 50, 318, 382, 383, 444, 461

Bowling Gough 36-5-149-5; Headley 25-2-125-2; Smith 23-2-89-0; Ealham 19-3-56-2; Croft 18-1-49-0; Butcher 2-0-14-0

Australia won by an innings and 61 runs
Umpires M J Kitchen and C J Mitchley
Toss Australia

Splits

		Lunch	Tea	Close
First day	England	9-0	14-0	106-3
Second day	England	172		
	Australia		114-4	258-4
Third day	Australia	373-5	–	–
Fourth day	Australia	501-9 dec		
	England		102-4	212-4
Fifth day	England	268-9	268	

I

First Day

My best memories of Headingley are the first ones. 1984 it was and I went there for the Friday and Saturday of the third Test against Clive Lloyd's great side of that summer, staying overnight at Morris's place. On my own on the Friday and never having been to the ground before, I took a cab from the station and I found myself at an entrance exclusively (I think it was) for ticket-holding Yorkshire members. But the guy on the gate who explained this to me also said that he happened to have a spare ticket for the Members' Enclosure and that if I wanted it I could have it. So I sat there happily the Friday, watching people ambling back and forth as they do on the perimeter track at Headingley and, beyond them, the progress of the match. Among the passers-by were members of the BBC commentary team and other cricketing notables, and in general I had a very nice day, striking up a friendship for the duration of it with a couple of the Yorkshire members sitting next to me.

This was the game in which Malcolm Marshall later particularly strutted his stuff. The thumb of his left hand fractured, he batted one-handed to keep Larry Gomes company to his hundred and then went on to bowl in the England second innings, the lower part of his left arm in plaster. He took the small matter of 7 for 53. Despite these heroics, I have another more personal memory of my first visit to Headingley. On the Saturday morning Morris and I got into the ground a little after play had already begun (a fact I shudder to have to reveal to my co-chronicler here), and Michael Holding was helping the West Indian tail to wag pretty vigorously, smiting the ball about as if batting were every bit as much his thing as gliding gracefully to the wicket with the poor batsman in his sights. Not long after we reach our seats and positioned near the boundary edge roughly behind long-on, I'm watching Holding set about him, and he strikes a huge blow up towards our end of the ground. I see at once that it is in my direction and, in the way these things happen – sort of slowly within the elongated moment – I have time to think that I may soon be put on my mettle to have to catch the ball. It's a shame I can't end the story by saying that I did have to and that I caught it. It isn't as good as that. Still, Holding's blow was a six, it fell across the boundary rope with a single bounce into my hands, and I proudly held on to it. Thus do we lesser mortals seek some small token of the glory that these others put before us on the field of play. On the BBC highlights of that evening if they are extant, you will be able to see, practically first thing Saturday morning, a small orange-looking blur where the ball arrives. The orange is of a coat I used to wear to cricket at the time and the blur is me.

My later memories of Headingley are less good. I watched England play the West Indies there again in 1988, and Pakistan in 1992, and for much of what I saw of those two games I was sitting on, or right next to, the Western Terrace. The less said about watching cricket from the Western Terrace the better. Let us confine it to the observation that it can sometimes be funny there but as often it isn't, and that the place is the dung-heap of cricket spectating, at least as this is known to me.

I have never, before now, been at Headingley to see England play Australia and so my memories of their contests there are, like most cricket memories, acquired from further away, through radio, TV and the press. One memory of Headingley in modern times stands out above all others, of course, and this is 1981. Botham, Willis and (not to forget his part in it) Brearley, and the most dramatic and astonishing turnaround in a game of cricket that could be imagined. So dominant is the memory of it in the English cricketing mind, however, that seemingly all that has happened at the same venue since then has been erased. In the run-up to this fourth Test the BBC advertises its coverage with images of Botham in that year, and in the official souvenir programme which I buy as I arrive at the ground, the 1981 Test at Headingley takes up most of the space allotted to memorable games played there, and this is then followed by a quick round-up of the 80 years before it. Nothing at all from afterwards. Me personally, I have this recollection that in 1989 Australia scored 601 for 7 declared and in 1993 they improved on it with 653 for 4 declared. They trounced England on both occasions. In 1989 Steve Waugh made a superb 177 not out and in 1993 Allan Border clocked up 200 not out. Oh yes and Waugh another 157 not out; the guy doesn't even have a calculable Test batting average for this ground. So 1981 is one thing, and these later games are another.

In the days before the Test, the history seems to become relevant in an indirect way, for there is discussion of the pitch to be used. A last-minute change has been made. It will not be the pitch relaid five years ago and on which Australia made those giant scores, but one of the earlier and less predictable strips. Words have been traded back and forth. Mark Taylor has suggested that it is inappropriate for the Test selectors to intervene in the choice of pitch. He wonders if England are perhaps running scared. Mike Atherton says it's all a fuss about nothing.

Neither here nor there. The game itself is the thing. We have had a longer break between Tests, mid-series, and the resumption seems to me long overdue. The first three games have nicely posed the question. What is the answer to be?

We are obliged to wait a while to find out. By four o'clock on the first day we've had only 20 minutes cricket, a mere four overs and five balls, the four overs before lunch and the five balls after it, and England are 14 for no wicket, having been put in to bat by Taylor, winning his fourth consecutive toss. There is not much more to say, either, about the rain which is the cause of this. A thin drizzle alternating with dryish spells before lunch gave way to a downpour of Lord's-like proportions immediately after it. Ian, Morris and I repaired to a covered stand on Headingley's rugby league ground, where we chatted until Morris had to leave for a doctor's appointment. One subject of discussion between us was Morris's exact alignment on the England-Australia partisanship spectrum. For 20 years, I must say, I have been taking this to be unambiguously pro-Australian, but it turns out that it is more nuanced: neutral and, in any case, interested in seeing good cricket; yet with a deal of respect for many of the Australian players. I fail to figure it out. I must talk further with him about it and try to win him back. Or is it win him over? When Morris leaves, Ian and I sit there writing and looking out at the cars parked neatly across the rugby league ground. An inspection by the umpires is due shortly after 4.00. We await developments.

In the end we got some cricket, 31 more overs and a little over two hours. A bonus for us was this. By the time play restarted at 4.50, many people had left the ground and there were gaps everywhere in the stands where earlier in the day there had been few. The stand in which we had been sheltering backs on to a section facing the cricket ground and reserved for Yorkshire members. Rather than going back to our seats in the North Enclosure, we evaded the check at one of the doors leading through to this section and watched the cricket from there. What an excellent location it is, above and behind the slips and close up to the play, better in this respect even than the seats we had at Lord's. Feeling a little uncomfortable for the first 10 minutes in case we should be discovered, we soon settled in once it became clear that no one was the least bit bothered.

We saw some well-contested and absorbing cricket. Butcher and Atherton were once again steady and careful, Atherton not getting off the mark indeed until the tenth over. They took the score past 40 before Butcher was unlucky to be out hitting a ball from Reiffel hard to Blewett at forward short leg, where it was taken as a reflex catch, clutched awkwardly to Blewett's body. Stewart, who has been having a poor run with the bat, continued it by popping up another catch to Blewett, this one simple, off Gillespie. He had made 7 and the score was 58 for 2. Atherton and Hussain then moved it along to 103, before Hussain was nicely taken at second slip by Taylor off McGrath. Sent in as night-watchman, Headley helped Atherton to see out the final overs.

As we were leaving, Ian and I debated Headingley's merits as a ground. The facilities are lousy – no public telephone in the whole place – and the leg-room is insufficient. But at least to look at, it has its own small-scale charm, crouching down among the houses. Ian, a hard man to please in these matters, doesn't agree. I came by train this morning, but I catch a lift back to Manchester with him. We reckon honours are even on the day, and so does Geoffrey Boycott. But Piwi in Hitchin thinks Australia haven't achieved quite enough in the conditions, whereas Ian Chappell thinks Australia just have the edge. Such is the science of cricket-watching.

Second Day

In a series that has already had some remarkable days, this one was absolutely riveting. It fell into either two or three distinct phases, depending on your principle of division. According to a first one, wickets tumbled for half the day, no fewer than 11 of them for only 116 runs; then they stopped tumbling and two batsmen, Matthew Elliott and Ricky Ponting, in the side in place of Bevan, stayed together in an unbroken partnership of 208. According to a second principle of division, the day was a bit like a sandwich. There was a great session for Australia in the morning, and another one over the last half of the day. Between these lay a brief and delectable flourish for England and their supporters. Whether two phases or three, today Australia may all but have settled the destiny of the Ashes.

Ian and I arrived at the ground in plenty of time after a comfortable drive over and one of the first things we saw was the aforesaid Geoffrey Boycott, on his way somewhere intent on business. Following our elevation of the previous afternoon, we returned to our seats in the North Enclosure, and for a brief period it looked as if England might build a reasonable innings, with Dean Headley knocking up a quick 22 and Atherton sticking in there, not playing at any delivery he didn't have to. In fact he had only two scoring shots in the same time. But it wasn't to last. Gillespie broke the partnership, getting Headley caught by Steve Waugh in the gully, and Australia didn't look back from there till lunch. For Atherton – incomprehensibly in view of the great care he had taken to this point – hooked a ball from McGrath down Gillespie's throat at long leg (at which point a guy behind us with a strong Midlands accent observed ruefully, 'They ain't got much brains north of Birmingham'), and Gillespie went on to destroy the England innings. He made a thorough mess of Thorpe's wicket, also bowled Gough and Smith, and he had Crawley and Croft caught, the first by Blewett after the ball had bounced up off his boot (shades of a famous incident from 1985), the second by Ponting leaping up at backward short leg to pluck the ball out of the air. It was all over five minutes before lunch, the last six wickets falling for 18 runs. England had made 172. Gillespie took six of the seven wickets to fall during the morning, and in catching Atherton he had had a hand in the other dismissal as well. His overall figures were 7 for 37, the best bowling performance by an Australian at Headingley. He had looked to me, even yesterday afternoon, the most threatening of the three Australian quick bowlers. Today he did the business. After McGrath's performance at Lord's, Warne's at Old Trafford and now Gillespie's here, my worry after Edgbaston about the quality of the Australian attack has been well and truly shown up. But an Aussie fast bowler wearing earrings... Who could have foretold it?

To say I was pleased by this turn of events would be an understatement. It was far better, and quicker, than I had expected. Still, with all the talk about the wicket, the anxiety was that Australia might find life just as tough. Taylor was gone – caught by Stewart off Gough – before either he or Australia had scored, though this in itself was no indication of anything in view of his appalling sequence of scores in the series to date. The century at Edgbaston aside, it now reads 7, 1, 2, 1, 0. Elliott began in adventurous fashion, striking a four and a six off Headley in quick succession, but when Blewett and the Waugh brothers were back in the pavilion with only 50 on the board – Blewett's wicket to Gough, the Waughs both to Headley – things were looking serious: like an England lead for sure, and possibly even another innings debacle as at Edgbaston. Considering that Elliott had been dropped by Thorpe off Smith the ball before Steve Waugh was out, the Australian situation at this point was parlous.

Ponting now joined Elliott, however, and they played their way safely to tea, adding 64 runs. 114 for 4 looked better. It offered hope that the Australian innings might come in somewhere close to England's. Wrong. The two young Australians stayed together throughout the last session of the day, batting with a combination of watchfulness and controlled aggression that completely changed the shape of the game. By close of play they had added 208 runs, passing, just on their own, the joint contribution of the entire England team. They exhibited a range of beautiful attacking shots, threw in a few sixes (Elliott another off Headley and one off Croft, Ponting one off Smith), and Elliott reached his second hundred of the series. Ponting was in sight of one himself, on 86. Just to set it down like that, though, the bare details, fails to capture the remarkable feel of this day's play. As the partnership mounted – past 100, then 150, exceeding the England total, towards 200 – one had to remind oneself that it was happening on the same day in which there had been a veritable clatter of falling wickets. By the end indeed, it was hard to escape the sense of having lived through something rather longer than a day. 11 wickets and 324 runs. And pretty well two-thirds of these runs Elliott and Ponting's. Their achievement was invaluable, a golden partnership. When they came together England were on the verge of establishing a winning position, and the two of them reversed things. If Australia can capitalise on what they did and win the game, their contribution to retaining the Ashes will be long remembered. Late in the day Elliott was dropped a second time, hooking; in this instance by Smith, the unfortunate bowler to Thorpe's earlier miss. But it mattered less now. Elliott's century, like the one at Lord's, was flawed thus by the chances he survived. Yet one had to admire the boldness of his play.

Another matter. My Spectating Award for the series so far goes to the segment of the Headingley crowd sitting in our vicinity in the North Enclosure. It was knowledgeable, fair-minded, good-humoured and funny, most prominent within it, for Ian and me, a group in the row behind – including the guy from Birmingham mentioned earlier and someone else with the good, standard-setting name of Norm – whose conversation we enjoyed through the day. Remarks on the misfortune of being an England supporter and the follies of the English batsmen followed upon tales of the greater and lesser misdemeanours of Graham Gooch. More generally the crowd at large, including the Western Terrace, comported itself well even by my stringent standards. Given what has gone before in the series, I may regret writing this, but anyway you read it here. To Headingley on the Friday: the Geras Spectating Award of the series to this point. Also: a young boy sitting next to Ian came by us and returned four times for four ice creams, which he consumed over no more than 45 minutes while maintaining both his composure and his well-being; for which the palm to him.

England are in grave trouble. I take nothing for granted but I hope the fates do not now pull a fast one. On the way home we stop at a pub to let the traffic thin out. I phone Adèle and discover that the weather is forecast to be bothersome again for the third day of this Test.

Third Day

Driving over from Manchester this morning, we paid close attention to the sky. The nearer we came to Leeds, the better things looked, the windscreen ever clearer. By the time we arrived at the ground we had reason to think we would see at least some play. And so we did. After watching Warne and Ponting for a while batting in the nets, we went to our seats and settled in, reading the morning papers to see what others had made of the remarkable events of yesterday.

Play duly began and, despite one ominous-looking period when a vast, dark cloud mass drifted across the ground, we got virtually a full first session, rain claiming only the last few minutes of it. In that session Australia consolidated their position, adding 115 more runs for the loss of Ricky Ponting, who had meanwhile completed a fine hundred. He comfortably outscored his partner this morning, Matthew Elliott rather less assured than yesterday. Ponting, back in the Australian side – and some had been wondering why he was ever dropped from it – had seized his chance. He played some sumptuous shots either side of getting to the century, two great cover drives amongst them. His innings was saluted by the crowd, who gave him a generous ovation both when he reached the hundred mark and when he was out. Having just struck several boundaries, he attempted a hook and mis-hit a ball from Gough high into the heavens, from where it descended into the hands of Mark Ealham at point. By then Ponting and Elliott had added 268 for the fifth wicket – after Bradman and Barnes in Sydney in 1946-47 (405), and Border and Waugh here in 1993 (332 unbroken), the third highest Australian fifth wicket partnership of all time. The only chance in Ponting's innings came after he had already reached his century. He danced down the wicket, missed a ball from Croft, and Stewart failed to gather it for the stumping. Ponting was on 109 and it cost England a further 18 runs from him. After he was out, Healy helped Elliott to add 55 more runs and Elliott took his score to 150.

During this morning Ian evidently felt the need to adjust his spectating mode. 'I think I'll just sit here and enjoy the stroke-play,' he said while Ponting was doing his stuff, 'I'll stop worrying about the Ashes.' By contrast, a young bloke sitting next to me, a Leeds United supporter, became more and more restive, plainly not much interested in anything going on on the field if it could not be the sight of England prospering. At one point he offered a semi-public reading from some tabloid, of bizarre and unlikely sexual facts. When I declined the beer he kindly offered me, he asked if I was 'just here for the cricket'.

Once the rain started, it didn't stop. Back to the covered stand in the rugby league ground, as on Thursday. We ate our lunch, and then got down to a couple of hot games of Scrabble, both of which, I'm happy to report, I won. This is some compensation for the humiliating side bet situation, where I continue to languish. Also to be recorded is that after only these two games, Ian and I have beaten the Geras family record for joint aggregate Scrabble score, formerly 702, now 710. Ian left some time before me, and when play was called off for the day towards 5.00 the rain was really chucking it down. I grabbed a taxi to Morris's, and for a good couple of hours that evening he, his son Andy and I vigorously debated all matters relating to the present series: whether Taylor, yesterday, was really out; whether Crawley was; the criminal irresponsibility of Graham Thorpe (according to Morris) for dropping Elliott; the idiocy of selecting a trundler – and no irony here – like Smith; and (the subject I liked best of these) the general quality of the Australian side, Mark Taylor's current batting miseries notwithstanding.

Fourth Day

A day as marvellous and changeable in its own way as Friday was. As then, the rain had pulled away to leave us all free to enjoy ourselves in the sunshine. As then, too, more than 300 runs were scored, 340 this time, and wickets fell regularly for a good portion of the day, eight of them in all. The quality of the day, though, lies in the fluctuation of Australian and English fortunes. By mid-afternoon, after Australia had declared at lunch on 501 for 9 and four top English batsmen were out with only 89 on the board, England looked dead and all but buried. But then Nasser Hussain played an innings of some courage and class given the situation facing his team, an example of chanceless batsmanship which ranks with the best of this series. With John Crawley as anchor at the other end, he took England to a position where they might just save the match and... thoughts even hover of 1981, although surely, here, impossibly. It was the kind of day which, like the Friday, makes Test cricket the greatest of games: each Test its own story, with its successive chapters, its dramas and its twists of plot, and all this against the backdrop of a longer and larger story. And it was the kind of day also, with that passage of English counter-attacking resistance, which makes the Ashes the premier, most keenly-felt and fought contest in all cricket.

I walked to the ground this morning, some 25 minutes from Morris's place. On my way I found an unopened can of Coke, which I decided to drink myself and not pass on to Ian as I had the packet of cigarettes at Lord's, in case doing so should again help England to a draw. At our seats, waiting for him to arrive, I noticed a strange ritual being played out in the middle. Not far away from the rest of the Australians at practice, Jason Gillespie appeared to be receiving instruction in running between the wickets. He would stand at one end of the out-of-use batting strip chosen as the site of his instruction, play a make-believe shot, then run to the other end, ground his bat and return. Another bloke, observing this, would then have a word with him and the whole would be repeated. It went on maybe 10 minutes. What could be the meaning of it?

As I wonder about that, an announcement comes over the public address system. It is to the following effect: Yorkshire County Cricket Club strongly disapproves of anti-social behaviour; spectators are advised to report any such to the stewards who will take appropriate steps. I am surprised. Have they somehow managed to read my account of the Edgbaston Test in which I advocate precisely this sort of policy? Has Ian been secretly selling copies of it, pre-publication? In any case I heartily approve, and I wonder how far it is the action of the Club that has produced such a good atmosphere at the ground so far. Later in the day, one on which there is a lot of useless and repetitive shouting a few rows behind us – as in 'Australia you're crap', or 'Gillespie (or McGrath) you're a wuss (or a woman)', loud, stupid, over and over again – I revert to my more usual grumpiness about this. But today at least, nothing can divert or detract for long from the contest going on out in the middle.

Australia came out to bat in the morning 201 runs ahead and I was hoping for a 300 lead. It looked at first as though we might not get that, Healy and Warne both going early for just 10 runs added, the former playing on to Ealham, the latter caught by Thorpe at slip off the same bowler. But Reiffel now helped Elliott to add a further 61 runs, and in the course of their partnership Elliott took his own individual score past the England total and began to approach the double century. There is a well-established set of expectations at such times. The batsman will notice his score and play with especial concentration. The field will be placed by the opposing captain to make it as difficult as possible for him to reach the landmark; to steal an easy single once that is what he needs. The spectators will watch this mini-contest within the contest and they will generally reckon on the batsman getting to win it in the end. At 199, just the one run wanted. Darren Gough knocks out Elliott's off stump and the crowd erupts. The thing that was least expected, though lurking there in the wings, has happened. People would happily have applauded the man's 200, and many will even be sympathetic that he didn't make it. But no quarter. It has to be earned and not conceded. It all helps, anyway, to adorn the history and lore of the game. How many batsmen in Test cricket has *this* befallen? I later dig up that only two have previously been out on 199: Mudassar Nazar for Pakistan against India, and Mohammed Azharuddin for India against Sri Lanka, both in the mid-1980s. It is a first between England and Australia.

Gough also bowls Jason Gillespie not long afterwards and when he returns to our corner of the ground to field, he is a hero to the crowd. Gough at Headingley, amongst his own. He is a battling, whole-hearted cricketer. You can see this in his bearing. You can see it especially from behind, in the shoulders, the lower back and the stout legs as he makes his way from one place to another. You see the determination, the eagerness to have the ball in his hand and to get at the batsman. The determination has an oddly mixed quality to my own eye. It is at once the attitude of the pace bowler plying his fearsome trade and – in Gough's case – an almost childish enthusiasm to compete, to play. It is there in the walk, which has something of the look about it of a slightly pugnacious toddler.

With these two wickets that give him 5 for 149, Gough also helps accomplish a first for me and Ian. It is the first time either of us has correctly chosen both best bowler and best batsman for the innings, and it is (naturally) me rather than Ian that has accomplished this. McGrath and Reiffel add another 40 runs for the ninth wicket and Australia go to lunch on 501. As expected, they declare.

England began their innings, and though runs immediately came at a fair lick, five an over, and no batsman was disposed of before showing signs of settling in, it soon appeared this might be another tale of English woe, a defeat without a fight. McGrath dismissed Butcher and Atherton in quick succession, Butcher caught behind by Healy, Atherton by Warne at slip. Modest partnerships then preceded the dismissals of Stewart, bowled by Reiffel, and Thorpe, caught off Gillespie by Mark Waugh after Healy, failing to take the ball, knocked it across toward him at second slip. England, now on 89 for 4, were in deep distress. But here is where Nasser Hussain played an innings that illuminated Headingley in the late Sunday sunshine, gave England supporters a growing corner of hope, and gave me, progressively, something to worry about. His composure was outstanding, his boundaries – 13 of them in the hundred – at once forthright and elegant. After the double century at Edgbaston this hundred, made under much more pressing circumstances, consolidates his stature as a batsman of real class. It was the latest variation on what is establishing itself as something of a theme in this series: the big innings forged in a difficult situation, whether personal or collective. That is Mark Taylor in his second innings at Edgbaston. It is Steve Waugh, twice, at Old Trafford. It is, then, Elliott and Ponting here at Headingley. And it is Hussain today. It is why people love cricket and the other great sports. It is the test of character, on public display.

Hussain and Crawley, the latter outshone but his role indispensable, passed the fifty, and later the hundred, partnership and were still together at the close, with the deficit reduced to 117. They have set things up for the final day. Australia will still be heavily favoured to win. But the draw is now a possibility somewhat less remote; and at the very margin, whether of hope or of disquiet, there is even... No, I refuse. There isn't.

Fifth Day

Despite the resistance of Hussain and Crawley yesterday, no one was giving England much chance of saving the game in the morning press. The general reaction seemed to be that, as well as the two of them had played, it was too little too late. In line with my usual pessimism, however, I was anxious in case they might somehow deny Australia. I again put a fiver on England to win, at odds this time that would have yielded serious consolation money – £750 – had they pulled off a miracle.

But the 'too-little-too-laters' were right. Not only did my anxieties prove groundless, the game didn't even run into the second half of the day; we were heading for home by about 2.00. The writing was on the wall when yesterday's man proved to be just that, lofting a straightforward catch off Warne to Gillespie at mid-off. It was a feeble end to a fine innings. Hussain had added four to his overnight score and one end would now be relatively open to the Australian bowlers. Ealham helped Crawley mount an hour's further resistance during which time he scored an extremely slow 4. He was caught absolutely brilliantly by Mark Waugh at second slip, off the bowling of Reiffel. The ball was already past Waugh and was going some; he shot out his right hand, seized it and, turning, gathered it safely to him. This was certainly the catch of the series so far. When Reiffel bowled Crawley minutes later for what had been a creditable 72, the sole question remaining was whether England could last till lunch. They could, but only just. Headley was lbw to Reiffel for 3 and Gough recorded a second duck, this one first ball, Mark Waugh picking up another very useful catch off Gillespie. That made it three in all to him in the innings. England went to lunch with nine wickets down.

We had enjoyed all this – well, I had anyway; Ian's feelings were doubtless more mixed – from the prime spectating position again, where we had been on the first afternoon. With so few people present for the final day, no one cared where people sat, in view of which it was a mystery why this part of the members' section wasn't full. While eating our lunch, we debated whether Croft and Smith could survive two overs – or maybe three. The answer was that they couldn't survive at all. Croft was out first ball after the interval, caught by Healy off Reiffel, to give the latter 5 for 49. England were out for 268 (suddenly an influential number: the margin, also, of Australia's victory at Old Trafford; the runs put on by Elliott and Ponting for the fifth wicket). Australia had won conclusively again.

Ian and I stayed long enough to see Gillespie chosen by Ian Botham as man of the match and we then set off back to Manchester. Australia are 2-1 up and have shown themselves to be the competitive professional outfit we thought they were before they arrived but started, wrongly, to have doubts about at Edgbaston. I believe the Ashes are now safe, though it needs a draw from one of the last two games of the series to clinch them. Going one Test ahead with Australia, I have gone 50p further behind on the side bets, to £2 down, the 50p equivalent to Ian's bonus for predicting England's second innings score within two runs. Attentive readers will remember that I have already settled for this distribution of fortunes. And they will not forget that I'm also 2-0 up at Scrabble.

The victory today makes it three consecutive decisive victories for Australia at Headingley: by 210 runs in 1989, an innings and 148 runs in 1993, and an innings and 61 runs in 1997. Time at last, perhaps, to put 1981 in its place – history. The image, in any event, that I think I will retain longest from this match is one I got, not at the ground itself, but only on returning home. I got it from the BBC highlights of the final day. It is of Waugh's wonderful catch to dismiss Mark Ealham. It is accompanied by the exclamations of Richie Benaud who, though always generous where praise is deserved, has by now seen too much to be easily surprised. His mere utterance of the name 'Mark Waugh' here says it all. But the thing I will remember, and cherish, more particularly, is the Australian fielders crowding around Waugh, unable to contain their admiration and delight. Shane Warne comes away from the now customary exchange of hugs and, beaming, puts his hands to his head for a moment as if to say, 'Did you *see* that?' It is a fitting image for the Australian mood after the winning cricket they have played over the last two Tests.

II

Thursday

On the eve of the Headingley Test, Norm and I found ourselves in the familiar situation of swapping weather forecasts. For pretty much the fourth time in four Tests, none was good. On this occasion, however, we had ample reason to feel aggrieved: for two weeks since the Old Trafford Test the weather had mainly been excellent. All part of the game, of course.

Cricketing debate in the run-up to the Leeds Test was dominated by two issues: Graham Gooch's decision to retire from first-class cricket, and a pitch-switching controversy at Headingley. Gooch's retirement had been announced on the day prior to the Test – his forty-fourth birthday – after a season of indifferent form, including only one score over 50. For me he will always be one of the great batsmen, though he is unlikely to rank with the immortals on any other count. The pitch-switching business had surfaced several days earlier when the decision was taken to use the reserve strip in place of the one originally prepared for the Test. The key question was who had taken the decision and, to be more precise, whether the central individual had in fact been David Graveney, chairman of the England selectors. Some pooh-poohed this suggestion. Some were only too happy to build a conspiracy theory around Graveney and an original strip alleged to be too 'Warne-friendly'. Some considered the whole story to be little more than media hype.

A further issue was of course debated as the Test approached: could England bounce back from the Old Trafford defeat? The view of the pundits was uniformly yes. Agnew, Benaud, Martin-Jenkins and others all argued that England could certainly win again in this series and, indeed, that their best chance of doing so was at Headingley. The view of the great British public seemed to be rather different. As Richie Benaud said on the *Today* programme on the morning of the first day, the only people who did not believe England could win at Headingley were England supporters. I have no doubt this statement was as accurate as all the others Richie makes about cricket. At work earlier in the week, the view that had gained widest assent when the pitch-switching controversy came up in conversation was that no pitch could ever suit England's bowlers over Australia's. It's an odd business this national sporting pessimism. I have to admit that going into the fourth Test I felt it to some extent too. Of course England played superbly at Edgbaston, and even came out of Lord's well enough in the end. Only at Old Trafford were they really exposed, so why should they now be written off as a spent force? I knew it was not wholly rational, but as a spent force was how it was all too easy to see them.

The journey to Leeds prompted pessimism of a different kind. As I drove across from Manchester rain clouds were actually sitting on the M62, not the sort of thing you like to see when you are travelling in search of cricket. On this first morning I didn't even get near Headingley till 11.00, but that didn't matter as it had been raining for at least the final half of my journey.

I went to the ground all the same and looked around. Headingley was the only one of the six Test venues that remained unknown to me, and it immediately struck me as the least impressive of the six. Like Edgbaston, Headingley seems to boast a cast-off football stand, except that here the Main Stand (of all things) really is a football stand, doubling up on its other side as a piece of the Leeds Rhinos' rugby league stadium. Like Old Trafford, Headingley has a certain flatness and lacks a pavilion looking wicket-to-wicket. Again, though, Headingley is the less satisfying venue because its flatness is strangely asymmetrical and its pavilion does not even look side on and has no players' balcony. All in all, it's an odd place.

Having taken the place in I sought out Norm and his friend Morris (joining us for the day). In keeping with the ground itself, our seats were the worst we had had so far: in the North Enclosure under the giant TV screen, but perilously close to the Western Terrace (home, according to Norm, to the Barmy Army). Again Taylor had won the toss – four in four – and would field. Atherton, it was later revealed, wanted to bat first anyway. Play had been rescheduled to commence at 11.50. England were giving a first cap to Gloucestershire's Mike Smith (leading wicket-taker in the County Championship) in place of Caddick. Australia had Ricky Ponting in for Bevan.

The players did in fact come out at 11.50, but no sooner had they done so than the rain returned. There was enough of it to drive the players back inside, but not enough to delay play for more than a short while. The start was re-rescheduled for 12.10. Norm and I placed our side bets. Ian: Stewart, Reiffel, 210. Norm: Hussain, McGrath, 247.

What followed was frustrating in a way peculiar to cricket: four overs before rain brought about an early lunch; a mainly dry interval to 1.25; five deliveries in light drizzle before slightly heavier rain took the players off again. Soon the rain was very heavy, though fortunately before the worst of it fell Norm, Morris and I had reached the protective cover of the Rhinos' stand (which does, after all, have its uses). We chatted for a while till Morris left. Thereafter Norm and I again rued our failure to bring a Scrabble set. In the morning session of four overs England had made 9 for 0 (Butcher 8, no ball 1). In the afternoon session of five deliveries they had added a further 5 for 0 (Butcher 1, byes 4).

Play eventually resumed just after 4.50: a further 31.1 overs could be (and in the event were) bowled, making a grand total of 36 in the day. Not so bad after all. It was, though, a strange closing session in which the issues of cricketing life and death which were at stake for some reason did not actually seem to be. I tried to figure out why. One factor was undoubtedly the anxiety brought on at the start of the evening session by our success in sneaking into the members' seats at the top of the Main Stand (which, with a view down the wicket from right on top of play, were the best we had sampled all series). Another was the competing interests of the crossword puzzlers seated behind us. 'It comes out meaning grim. Mac for Scotsman, AB for sailor, RE for about. Macabre!' Then: 'Kitsch.' 'Quiche?' 'No, kitsch! I know that's what it is, I just don't know how to spell it. K-I-T-C-H-E is it?' Then again: 'Those two are certainly wrong if New Jersey's right.' 'New Jersey's right!' 'So what did you put those two in for?' 'It wasn't me, it was Terry.' 'Terry, what've you been doing here? You just put in anything you like!' A further factor was the unexpectedly gentle rumble coming off the Western Terrace (only one streaker all session). A final one was the surreal sight of Taylor turning to Greg Blewett for a three-over spell towards the end of the day when England could still have been put under considerable pressure. Blewett went for 17 runs.

Still, despite all this, real cricket did take place on the field as

England progressed to 106 for 3 by the close. The start they made was excellent and largely untroubled, partly because neither McGrath nor Reiffel found the right line or length. However, on 43 the fates intervened – or were conjured up by Norm? – when Butcher, who had played well for 24, struck a ball from Reiffel firmly into Blewett's midriff at forward short leg and saw it stick. 43 for 1, and a very unfortunate dismissal. Stewart – 103 runs at 20.6 in the series to date – came and went, also caught by Blewett (for 7), though this catch was a dolly and came off Gillespie. I've no idea why I took Stewart as my side-bet batsman. England 58 for 2. Hussain looked good for his 26 until McGrath found an edge towards the end of the day and Taylor took a superb slip catch immediately in front of us. England 103 for 3.

That dismissal, Norm and I agreed as we left the ground, had evened things up on the day. Atherton was still there on 34, with nightwatchman Headley on 0. We thought 250 would be a good total in the conditions and that England had a decent chance of getting there. The fourth Test was evenly balanced.

In the Geras household over dinner there was more lucky stone talk as Jen revealed she hadn't engaged in any polishing for the first day. Something to do with safeguarding the powers for a crucial occasion. 'But this is a crucial occasion!' objected Norm. 'Whoever loses this Test can kiss the Ashes goodbye.' My suggestion that the stone's powers be rested for the time being and then put to proper use after an England victory at Headingley was not viewed with favour by Norm. 'Don't listen to him!' The fourth Test is a matter of life and death after all.

Friday

All to play for was also the opinion of most commentators as the fourth Test moved into its second day. A few eccentrics considered one side or the other to have a marginal advantage, but unusually neither Norm nor I was other than entirely orthodox. By the day's close, the even balance of the first day had, however, been ruthlessly destroyed by Australia. It was, by any measure, an extraordinary day's cricket. In roughly the first half, 11 wickets fell for 116 runs. In roughly the second half, no wickets fell for 208 runs. Sadly for me, seven of the 11 wickets were English and 258 of the 324 runs were

Australian. By close of play England had been dismissed for 172 and Australia were 258 for 4. Another innings side bet victory for me, but otherwise not a good lookout. As we left the ground even Norm conceded that Australia were in a pretty good position, 86 runs to the good with six first-innings wickets standing. They sure were.

The odd thing is that the morning started quite brightly for England as nightwatchman Dean Headley hit a confident 22 runs before being out, caught Steve Waugh (in the gully), bowled Gillespie (off his first delivery of the morning). 138 for 4. Headley had certainly done a good deal more than could have been expected of him. It was the next dismissal that turned out to be the killer, and even appeared so at the time. Atherton, having played watchfully for 223 minutes and 142 balls (and indeed having played only two scoring shots – for four and three – in more than an hour's play on the day), inexplicably hooked ball number 143 (from McGrath) and was duly caught by Gillespie at long leg for 41. England 154 for 5. The floodgates then opened, or rather were prised apart by Gillespie, who in a magnificent spell of fast bowling from the Kirkstall Lane End demolished the rest of the England order. Thorpe, having pulled a couple of shortish deliveries for four, tried much the same with a fuller delivery and merely succeeded in clattering the ball into his stumps. Thorpe out for 15. England 154 for 6. Crawley, yet more unfortunate than Butcher, played a firm shot on to Blewett's toe and saw it bounce up into the fielder's hands. Crawley out for 2. England 163 for 7. Three wickets – England's final three – then fell on 172: Croft brilliantly caught by Ponting for 6, Gough and Smith each bowled for 0 by the second delivery they faced. England's innings closed some five or six minutes before lunch, the last six wickets having gone for 18. Gillespie finished with 7 for 37. It was uncannily like the third morning at Lord's. There England lost 7 wickets for 39 and McGrath finished with 8 for 38. Here they lost 7 wickets for 66 and Gillespie finished with 7 for 37. If anything, Gillespie's spell was the more hostile of the two.

It was sobering stuff, though as much for Norm as for me. After all Ian, if this can happen to England... The talkative and witty Brummie seated behind us captured my mood. Announcer (at the end of a catalogue of information): 'Enjoy your lunch interval.' Brummie: 'Enjoy your lunch interval? How can you when you're an England supporter!' Long faces around the ground indicated that he had his finger pretty firmly on the pulse of the nation. As the players reappeared for the afternoon session Norm and I made our Australian innings selections. Norm: Elliott, Gough, 247. Ian: Blewett, Headley, 289. We also bet on Taylor's score in the second innings. Ian 37, Norm 11. Bets worth £1 if exact, 50p if within a 10-run range, otherwise off.

That issue, like Hussain's final-session score on the second day at Old Trafford, was soon settled. Taylor was not dismissed for his customary 1 or 2, but for 0, caught by Stewart off a glove which failed to evade a Gough bouncer. Australia 0 for 1 (the first time such a score had been registered in the series). As in the England innings, the captain's dismissal opened a floodgate or two. Blewett was also caught by Stewart off Gough, for 1. Australia 16 for 2. Headley then picked up the Waugh twins: Mark caught and bowled for 8, Steve caught by Crawley at short leg for 4. Australia 43 for 3 and 50 for 4. Renewed hope. Indeed, the delivery prior to Steve Waugh's dismissal Elliott had been dropped at first slip by Thorpe off an eminently catchable head-high chance conjured up by the debutant Smith. Would Australia make it to 100? Norm certainly feared they might not.

He needn't have worried. Following a match score to this point of 222 for 14, Elliott and Ponting put together their unbroken stand of 208 by the close, averaging around four runs per over throughout. This in a match which had not previously seen a partnership amass more than the 45 put together by Atherton and Hussain. Unforgivably, England made a decisive contribution to the Elliott-Ponting partnership by putting down Elliott three times: on 29 (Thorpe off Smith), 63 (Atherton – a sharp chance – off Ealham) and 132 (Smith off Gough). More echoes of the recent past: Elliott's century at Lord's was by no means chanceless. That said, he made the most of his chances, striking three sixes and 17 fours in his undefeated 134 by the close. At the other end Ponting played beautifully and brilliantly, striking one six and 11 fours in a chanceless 86 not out. His flamboyant forward lunge at balls which he has no intention of playing will, however, surely become his trademark. The obvious parallel here was not at all comforting. At Edgbaston Australia's first innings of 118 was initially met with an England response of 50 for 3. 168 for 13 in the match, then, when Hussain and Thorpe came together to put on 150 by the close of the first day, and 288 in total. Although in that match Australia fought back strongly in their second innings, they still lost by nine wickets.

Sobering then, but also exhilarating from a non-partisan point of view. Like the first day at Edgbaston (318 runs and 13 wickets), the second day at Headingley had been packed with incident (324 runs and 11 wickets). And the atmosphere was superb: a great crowd in our section of the ground (with the exception of a misery in front who complained about the girls who inadvertently brushed ice cream against his shirt); only two streakers; and no more than limited activity from the fabled Western Terrace. Just before tea there was a small amount of Mexican waving, but that was the extent of it.

Meanwhile, England were not waving but drowning.

Saturday

The English obsession with the weather is one of the better-known national stereotypes. On days like those on which the fourth Test took place, that stereotype is easily understood. Following a second day of sunshine and friendly, fluffy clouds, the third day dawned wet and was, indeed, forecast to stay that way. We managed very nearly a full session before lunch – 28.2 overs – but then a persistent drizzle (with stronger stuff occasionally mixed in) established itself and stayed with us for the rest of the day.

In those overs Australia continued to pile on the agony for England, moving from 258 for 4 to 373 for 5. 115 for 1 on the day at a whisker above four runs per over. The one wicket to fall was Ponting's, the product of slight over-confidence (and who could blame him?) which resulted in a sliced hook to Ealham off Gough. Amazingly, given England's catching record in this match (and series), Ponting had already started his walk to the dressing room before Ealham had safely taken the catch. On the day Ponting had moved from 86 to 127 (in 202 balls), his first Test century. On 109, when the Australian score was 297 for 4, he had survived an easy stumping chance off Croft: further ammunition for those who bemoan England's persistence with a non-specialist wicket-keeper. I am one of those people.

318 for 5 when Ponting went, to close a partnership of 268. 'Just as we were looking good, a catastrophe!' joked Norm. He must have been feeling confident. Healy reinforced the point by stroking his first ball for four. Neither he nor Elliott looked troubled in the remainder of the day's play. Elliott had taken his score to 164 by the close. Healy was on 27.

As the rain set in Norm and I sloped off to the Rhinos' stand for cover. More newspaper reading for a bit, including further enjoyment of a sentence in Martin Johnson's *Telegraph* column which we had already read before the start of play: 'The innings of the [second] day, however, was played by Mike Smith, who lasted two balls, both of which involved footwork designed to offer Gillespie the clearest possible view of all three stumps'. More chat. Also some Scrabble, which this time we had thought to bring and could now put to good use. In the two games we played in the afternoon session Norm won 2-0. 341-296 in the first (in which Norm profited from the eccentric Scrabble rule that seven-letter words generate a 50-point bonus), 393-317 in the second. By 4.00 it was clear that rain would fall for the duration. I made my way out of the ground and returned to Manchester.

Sunday

As the fourth Test moved into its fourth day England were staring down both barrels, as one of the commentators (Christopher Martin-Jenkins on Radio 4?) put it. If the evidence of the first three days was anything to go by, this was likely to become a familiar state of affairs. But at least the weather had turned around again, and even as an England fan I was grateful for that.

First blood was actually drawn by England: in his first full over of the morning – that is, not the four balls bowled to complete the over held over from Saturday – Ealham bowled Healy for 31 and had Warne caught by Thorpe for 0. Australia 383 for 7. It was too early to run any new permutations, and in my case just good after so much punishment to savour *some* English success.

It turned out to be short-lived. Reiffel stepped out to join Elliott, and the carnage continued at a rate of around six runs per over throughout the morning session. The next success was in some senses regrettable even from an English perspective. Elliott in the 190s was looking twitchy. Just after Norm had informed me that someone – he could not remember who – at some point in the history of Test cricket had been out for this score, Elliott himself was bowled off stump by a superb yorker from Gough for 199. From one perspective you had to feel for Elliott. From another you could not help but recall that he could and should have gone for 29 (and 63 and 132). Maybe being out for 199 was not such an ordeal after all. Australia 444 for 8.

Gillespie didn't last long, being bowled by Gough for 3. Australia 461 for 9. With the lead now 289, we debated whether Taylor should declare and give his bowlers 20-30 minutes before lunch to start on the English batsmen. One issue that weighed with us was the fact that Australia's remaining batsman was McGrath, one of the international game's confirmed number elevens with a batting average of less than 4.

True to form, Taylor chose to bat on. Demoralisation was evidently still a key objective. And why not try to amass the series' first innings total of 500? Against all expectations, McGrath seemed highly capable of dealing with the English attack. Before too long 500 loomed into view. In the final over of the session it was reached, and indeed surpassed. The Australians took lunch on 501 for 9, with Reiffel on 54 (for a series average of 131) and McGrath on 20. Their unbroken partnership for the tenth wicket had put on 40 and taken the lead to 329. Australia's first four wickets having yielded 50 runs, their next five had chipped in 451. That, surely, was demoralising enough. In the break Taylor took the point and declared.

The early part of England's attempt to score the 329 (and more) needed to save the game conformed to the character of most of what had gone before: Butcher caught Healy bowled McGrath 19; Atherton caught Warne bowled McGrath 2; Stewart bowled Reiffel 16; Thorpe caught Mark Waugh (off a chance that was parried by Healy in front of first slip and picked up at second) bowled Gillespie 15. England at the end of all this 89 for 4. Then, thankfully and at last, things took a turn for the better as Crawley held down one end while Hussain built an excellent and substantial innings at the other. In the 90s he experienced the familiar heebie-jeebies, but nevertheless made it to a very fine century just before the close. By then England were 212 for 4, with Hussain on 101 and Crawley on 48. If England secure nothing else from this match, there is at least Hussain's innings to savour.

The only downside for me was the conditions in which we watched this phase of the match. The Western Terrace actually kept itself largely to itself, staging side shows which were mainly incomprehensible from our seats. Just occasionally a Mexican wave flowed past us before coming to grief at the point where the North Enclosure meets the Yorkshire CCC offices. Once or twice 'Stand up if you hate Man U' drew support from right round the western and northern stretches of the ground. But that, on the whole, was that. Unfortunately, however, we had our own partisans – mainly of Warrington and Washington (in the North East) – who droned on behind us for much of the afternoon and evening sessions. Twice the stewards calmed things a bit, though on neither occasion for long. Norm and I thought of moving seats, but in the event didn't.

What, then, might the final day bring? For my money Australia were still odds-on favourites, the draw looked like about a 5 to 1 chance and an England victory about 100 to 1. It also struck me that if England were to lose here – and surely thereby fail to regain the Ashes – the Mark Taylor question could be supplanted (or joined) by a Michael Atherton question. Indeed, it seemed from a glance at the *News of the World* being read in the row in front of us that this question was already on the agenda. The headline said something like 'Get rid of the wallies, bring on the Hollies' (that is, Surrey's Hollioake brothers), though whether the large picture of a despairing Atherton implied an attack on his position as captain I could not tell.

That, however, was for the future. At the end of day four England were still in the game (and series), and that in itself was something to be pleased about.

Monday

Norm and I set ourselves two tasks on reaching the ground on the fifth day. The first was to check the bookies' odds on the match. Ladbrokes' offerings were largely in line with the way it looked to me: Australia 1 to 5, the draw 3 to 1, England 150 to 1. Norm, who has a habit of donating large amounts of money to indigent bookmakers, placed a fiver on England to win. The second task was to break into the Main Stand and secure seats near those we had so liked on the first afternoon. This turned out to be entirely unproblematic, as there were no restrictions on entry even to the members' enclosure. We cheerfully took the best seats in the house, and settled to reading the papers. Most held the Hussain-Crawley partnership of the previous afternoon to be no more than a pleasant diversion. My thoughts entirely. The weather was certainly not going to intervene: although overcast, the skies did not look rain-bearing.

Once again on the field, England conjured up few surprises. Indeed, the only one I can think of is the rapidity of their pre-lunch collapse, which even for this England side in this match was greater than expected: from 252 for 5 at around 12.30 to 268 for 9 by lunch. The afternoon session turned out entirely as expected. Reiffel ran in to deliver the first ball of the session, Croft flapped at it, and Healy pocketed the catch. Before all that, England's hero of the fourth day, Hussain, had gone quickly – caught Gillespie bowled Warne – for 105. Crawley and Ealham then stuck around for over an hour to induce a small element of anxiety among Australians. However, when Ealham was brilliantly caught one-handed by Mark Waugh at second slip off Reiffel for 4 after 67 minutes and 47 balls of resistance (one of the slowest 4s in Test match history?), the collapse began in earnest. Crawley was bowled by Reiffel for 72. Headley was clearly lbw to Reiffel for 3. Gough, having been out second ball in the first innings, was out first ball in the second, sharply caught by Mark Waugh in the slips off Gillespie. England all out for 268 meant an Australian victory by an innings and 61 runs. Crushing indeed. At least it meant that while Norm had picked Hussain as top batsman I had come close enough to guessing the innings total – just two runs out – to win £1. My advantage in series side bets now stood at £2. We saw Gillespie named man of the match by Ian Botham and left. The weather was getting better and better.

Again that question surfaced: where next for England? Only Smith is certain to go. Only Atherton, Hussain, Gough and Headley look entirely secure. As for the other six, a case can be made for all of them. Butcher has done little wrong and increasingly looks the part. Stewart has a long history of achievement. Thorpe is a class act and took a century off the Australians at Edgbaston. Crawley has scored 83 and 72 in the last two Tests. Ealham averages 30-odd with the bat and 20-odd with the ball in the series. Croft has the makings of a good spinner. And yet question marks hang over each and every one of these players. My feeling is that some change must be made to the top of the order – which since the first Test has been the foundation for first innings scores of 77, 162 and 172 – and that Thorpe is the most obvious sacrifice. I have also long wanted to see Russell back in the England side, and that switch is now overdue. And surely Croft must join Smith in stepping down.

There is, however, a deeper conundrum, which is why England have been in such a cricketing rut for the past few years. In this Test

Thorpe's failure to take the catch that would have dismissed Elliott for 29 was held by some to be critical. Yet it seems highly unlikely that it was anything of the kind. Even if that chance had been accepted Australia would probably have found another way to win, if not by an innings then at least by a decent amount. In the *Guardian* Frank Keating had a wonderful piece about national character, which he illustrated with comments on the Hussain-Crawley partnership: 'To the English, self-deprecating and enjoying the black humours of real life, when the pressures are off and we have as good as lost it is time to begin to play some heavenly strokes. Just to show we can do it as well as anyone else – as long as it does not matter all that much. Nor does it really'. But how can this be true of the 1990s and not, say, of much of the 1980s (and earlier decades)? And anyway, is it true of the 1990s? I very much doubt it.

England have to win at Trent Bridge and the Oval to regain the Ashes. They will make changes, possibly more than are warranted. They seem highly unlikely to find a winning formula.

Fifth Test
Trent Bridge
7-10 August

Scorecard

Australia

M T G Elliott c Stewart b Headley	69	(2)	c Crawley b Caddick		37
*M A Taylor b Caddick	76	(1)	c Hussain b B C Hollioake		45
G S Blewett c Stewart b B C Hollioake	50		c Stewart b Caddick		60
M E Waugh lbw b Caddick	68		lbw b Headley		7
S R Waugh b Malcolm	75		c A J Hollioake b Caddick		14
R T Ponting b Headley	9		c Stewart b A J Hollioake		45
†I A Healy c A J Hollioake b Malcolm	16		c Stewart b A J Hollioake		63
S K Warne c Thorpe b Malcolm	0		c Thorpe b Croft		20
P R Reiffel c Thorpe b Headley	26		c B C Hollioake b Croft		22
J N Gillespie not out	18		c Thorpe b Headley		4
G D McGrath b Headley	1		not out		1
Extras (b 4, lb 10, w 1, nb 4)	19		(b 1, lb 11, nb 6)		18
Total (121.5 overs)	427		(98.5 overs)		336

Fall of wickets 117, 160, 225, 311, 325, 355, 363, 386, 419

51, 105, 134, 156, 171, 276, 292, 314, 326

Bowling *First Innings* Malcolm 25-4-100-3; Headley 30.5-7-87-4; Caddick 30-4-102-2; B C Hollioake 10-1-57-1; Croft 19-7-43-0; A J Hollioake 7-0-24-0 *Second Innings* Malcolm 16-4-52-0; Headley 19-3-56-2; Croft 26.5-6-74-2; Caddick 20-2-85-3; B C Hollioake 5-1-26-1; A J Hollioake 12-2-31-2

England

*M A Atherton c Healy b Warne	27	c Healy b McGrath	8
†A J Stewart c Healy b Warne	87	c S R Waugh b Reiffel	16
J P Crawley c Healy b McGrath	18	c Healy b Gillespie	33
N Hussain b Warne	2	b Gillespie	21
G P Thorpe c Blewett b Warne	53	not out	82
A J Hollioake c Taylor b Reiffel	45	lbw b Gillespie	2
B C Hollioake c M E Waugh b Reiffel	28	lbw b Warne	2
R D B Croft c Blewett b McGrath	18	c McGrath b Warne	6
A R Caddick c Healy b McGrath	0	lbw b Warne	0
D W Headley not out	10	c Healy b McGrath	4
D E Malcolm b McGrath	12	c M E Waugh b McGrath	0
Extras (b 2, lb 6, nb 5)	13	(b 6, lb 2, nb 4)	12
Total (93.5 overs)	313	(48.5 overs)	186

Fall of wickets 106, 129, 135, 141, 243, 243, 272, 290, 290

25, 25, 78, 99, 121, 144, 150, 166, 186

Bowling *First Innings* McGrath 29.5-9-71-4; Reiffel 21-2-101-2; Gillespie 11-3-47-0; Warne 32-8-86-4 *Second Innings* McGrath 13.5-4-36-3; Reiffel 11-3-34-1; Gillespie 8-0-65-3; Warne 16-4-43-3

Australia won by 264 runs
Umpires D R Shepherd and C J Mitchley
Toss Australia

Splits

		Lunch	Tea	Close
First day	Australia	84-0	181-2	302-3
Second day	Australia	405-8	427	
	England		76-0	188-4
Third day	England	272-7	313	
	Australia		56-1	167-4
Fourth day	Australia	278-6	336	
	England		25-1	186

I

First Day

Today was Adèle's and my thirtieth wedding anniversary. This is not particularly relevant except that 30 not out is, in such matters, quite a high score these days, high scores were in the news, and I associate Nottingham with flat, easy pitches and batsmen having a pretty good time of things.

High scores were in the news because of what had been happening in Colombo in the Test between Sri Lanka and India. The Sri Lankans had just beaten the record innings total for a Test match, one which had stood for nearly 60 years. They finished a drawn game on 952 for 6, thereby eclipsing the 903 for 7 declared England had made at the Oval in 1938, and two of their batsmen putting together the highest Test partnership of all time in the process. The night before this Test, also, I had done some hurried research on England versus Australia at Trent Bridge. While I didn't find what I expected to, a run of massive scores, there have certainly been some notable occasions there of that kind. There was the match in 1938, when England made 658 for 8 declared and Australia two totals of more than 400, producing, inevitably, a draw. It included five centuries and two double centuries. Stan McCabe made 232, the innings during which Bradman is said to have called his players out on to the balcony, advising them, 'You may never see its like again'. There is too, from more recent memory, the game in 1989 when Mark Taylor and Geoff Marsh batted through the whole of the first day in an unbroken partnership of 301. It ended on 329 the following morning and Taylor himself went on to score 219 in a total of 602 for 6 declared.

It is such high-scoring thoughts I was thinking, and talking about to Ian, as we arrived at the ground bright and early, having set out from Manchester just before 7.30. I first came to Trent Bridge in 1966 with Dick Fletcher, for the fourth day of the Test against the West Indies. *Wisden* reminds me that on that visit I saw Basil Butcher make 209 not out and share a partnership of 173 with Gary Sobers in a couple of hours, but for some reason I don't have as good a memory of this as I do of Sobers' earlier match-saving partnership with David Holford at Lord's. For once, anyway, Ian and I agreed: Lord's apart, Trent Bridge is the most attractive of the venues we have yet been to this summer. The approach to the ground itself is special, the Trent stretching away beside you as you cross the bridge with other expectant cricket-goers. And, inside, the place has a rather homely aspect: spectators are close up to the play and the stands blend together better than at Edgbaston, Old Trafford or Headingley. We were sitting in the Hound Road Stand (Lower), and it was a day of sweltering heat. Before lunch we were lucky enough to be protected by early shadow, and during the afternoon sessions we dodged as much of the sun as we could by taking the seats of the corporate guys, who seem to attend Test matches mostly for other reasons than to watch them, remaining absent from their seats for much of the day. More fool them but, on this occasion, lucky us. Another novel feature of our day, together with the intense heat, was that at lunch-time we paid a visit to the Press Box. We were seeking out, and found, Martin Johnson – with Matthew Engel and Frank Keating, the most entertaining of the writers commenting on the present series – who had kindly agreed to look at a couple of our Test accounts.

For the first time in the series Ian was present with me to see Atherton and Taylor toss for innings. We studied their reactions to see if we could tell the result before it was announced, and it was obvious: Taylor had called correctly – for the fifth time in a row. Predictably he chose to bat, and it wasn't long before my thoughts of high scores at Trent Bridge began to seem very much to the point. Although there were one or two instances of playing and missing or of awkwardness in the batsman's shot, this was the only first innings of the summer so far where the opening pair on day one seemed to settle early and offer promise of a big first-wicket partnership. The promise was duly delivered on. By lunch, Taylor and Elliott were still together with 84, and not long afterwards they had taken Australia to 100 without loss. Elliott was then out for 69, caught by Stewart off Headley with the total on 117. But Blewett in his turn gradually settled in with Taylor. He was uncertain and out of touch for a while, but the Australian captain was looking as good as he has since the start of the series, including in the century he made at Edgbaston. For the first time he came to seem totally assured, striking some clean and handsome boundaries. When he passed 61 he became the sixth batsman (with Border, Boon, Greg Chappell, Bradman and Harvey) to score 6000 runs for Australia, and he was surely well set by now for another century. On 76, however, and with the Australian total 160, Taylor was bowled by a beautiful ball from Caddick. Well pitched up, it sliced between bat and pad to uproot his off stump, disproving a hypothesis of Ian's that, having reached double figures, Taylor was bound to get a hundred, since he'd been turning in only single-figure and three-figure scores.

Mark Waugh joined Blewett and the two of them took Australia to 181 for 2 by tea and, after tea, to 225. Blewett had just reached his 50, growing in confidence as his innings proceeded and hitting some good-looking boundaries, when he played a loose shot outside off stump to Ben Hollioake and was well caught behind by Stewart. Ben and his brother Adam were making their debut together – to some public interest and media hype – but their bowling on this easy pitch had looked pretty innocuous up to this point. Those other brothers, the Waughs, were now brought together and they, for their part, batted with obvious comfort. Mark began to look at times like the batsman we know him to be, displaying some examples of that characteristic flick to the mid-wicket boundary which he brings off with no effort at all. When he reached his half-century, he was the fourth consecutive batsman at the top of the Australian order to do so. Meanwhile Steve was playing with his usual business-like approach, and he treated us to a couple of those blistering shots square on the off-side, one of which dissected the space between two neighbouring England fielders, neither of whom had time so much as to move before the ball crossed the boundary rope. As things drew towards close of play Ian, alluding to that first day of the Test here in 1989, said: 'I bet they finish on 301'. He was nearly right. At stumps Australia were 302 for 3. Another step nearer to taking the Ashes home.

Second Day

It was a scorching day again, which we spent keeping out of the sun. We have this down to a fine art already and are exposed for no more than an hour. When we arrived this morning, the mysterious practice that I'd witnessed at Headingley, with Gillespie apparently receiving instruction in running between the wickets, had been extended. Four Australians were now at it, supervised as before by this other bloke. Ian and I debated its significance, weighing what there was to be said for the notion that it was simply a form of fitness training, against my alternative hypothesis that the purpose was psychological: to fix it deep in Australian minds that what Australians did was to make runs, many runs, and that this hurrying back and forth, bat in hand, was simply what had to be done as a matter of routine. Whatever the case, my dream of a mammoth Australian total evaporated in the morning heat, and I had to make do merely with a big total. Who can fathom the vagaries of cricket? On a wicket which the entire national press is describing as shirt-front, featherbed, batsman's paradise and so forth and on which yesterday only three wickets fell for 302 runs, no batsman has yet reached 100 and today 11 wickets fell, albeit for another 313 runs.

It began early. Mark Waugh had played two relaxed leg-glances to the boundary, thereby taking his score to 68, and was then lbw to Caddick. The century which had been awaited from him all series, its best opportunity surely now, once more contrived to stay away. That was 311 for 4, and it set off a series of comings and goings. Ponting played on to Headley for 9, Healy was caught at slip by Adam Hollioake off Malcolm for 16, and Warne didn't trouble the scorers at all, also caught at slip off Malcolm, this time by Thorpe low to his right. Through it all, only Steve Waugh remained constant. He became the fifth batsman at the top of the Australian order to reach the half-century. He played two crashing square drives for four off an over from Ben Hollioake and, later, another off Devon Malcolm. But he too, just like his four predecessors in the innings, perished before getting to the hundred, his off stump crisply removed by a fine ball from Malcolm. He had made 75 and it was 386 for 8, a scoreline England supporters wouldn't have dared hope for at the start of the day.

Somewhere around here, a huge dragonfly passed by in front of us, as impressive a creature of its kind as I can remember seeing, and quite unconcerned by the question as to why no one making 50 in this match could get to 100. On 405 for 8, Australia went to lunch, having just passed the point – 402 – up to which I would have got 50p from Ian rather than him getting 50p from me. No matter. I wanted the runs. But Australia lasted only a further 25 minutes and 22 runs after lunch, Headley disposing of both Reiffel and McGrath. Australia were all out for 427 (by a numerical quirk, one of their two totals from that 1938 Test), and I was miserably cheated of a second 50p for bowler, as Headley leapt from two wickets to four, across Malcolm's three. £3 down now. And not the remotest prospect of Scrabble.

The highlights of the afternoon were Alec Stewart's batting and Shane Warne's bowling. Stewart played the kind of innings we have not before seen from him this series – combative, utterly dominant, threatening to take the bowlers apart. The sixth score now of 50 or more in this game, his was the best of them. It contained 10 boundaries as he passed the half-century mark, and while he was there England's scoring rate reached and exceeded four runs per over. Together with Atherton – quite overshadowed – Stewart compiled on either side of tea the second century opening partnership of the game. In a single over from Gillespie he struck 18 runs and the man (so recently) of the match at Headingley had to be removed by his captain from the line of fire. However, just when England were looking as if they might position themselves to make a serious assault on the Australian total, another logic came into play here, with the bowling genius of Shane Warne. In an unbroken spell of 22 overs, also on both sides of tea, Warne conjured three key dismissals and, with one thrown in from McGrath, it gave the England innings an entirely different aspect. From 106 for 0 it declined to 141 for 4.

Atherton was first to go, for 27, edging one from Warne to Ian Healy. Stewart's dismissal, 20-odd runs later, was formally the same – caught Healy bowled Warne – but more remarkable. Healy knocked the ball up over his head, then turned and dived a long way back behind him to take it just before it hit the ground. Umpire David Shepherd, unsighted, had to confer with Cyril Mitchley at square leg, but there was no doubt it was a clean catch; Ian and I could see this even from where we sat. Of the batsmen making 50 Stewart, at 87, had not only come closest to the century, he had looked the most certain to get there. Warne was bowling, however, and when he is, nothing is quite certain. Hussain was third to go, for only 2, beaten by a terrific, turning delivery that evaded his bat to hit off stump. The batsman lingered somewhat as if not quite sure of what had happened to him; or as if a shadow of that celebrated Gatting dismissal at Old Trafford in 1993 had just passed over Trent Bridge. Then Crawley was taken leg-side by Healy off McGrath – another excellent catch by this brilliant keeper – and the England situation was close to disaster. If Thorpe, getting off the mark, hadn't survived a run-out decision by the very skin of his teeth, a disaster is what it would have become. Thorpe tried a quick run and, in a wonderful piece of gathering and throwing, Gillespie hit the stumps at the bowler's end. It took the TV replay to show that Thorpe had either just made it or else not clearly enough failed to make it, so deserving the benefit of the doubt. He and Adam Hollioake managed to steady things and get England to 188 for 4 by close of play.

During their partnership, a number of pigeons – maybe a dozen, perhaps a few more – serenely pecked away in the area between mid-on and mid-wicket (that is, with the bowling from the Pavilion End). Quite untroubled when either the ball or a fielder in pursuit of it sped by them, they went about their business of the afternoon. Their judgement of the ball's path seems to be immaculate and they know more or less what to expect from the humans nearby. Otherwise, they take no more interest in the cricket than the dragonfly.

Third Day

The weather continues hot and the cricket competitive. As the morning papers were telling us 'hottest day of the year', Ian and I stuck to our seat-hopping strategy to keep in the shade, but today for the first time we suffered a serious setback. Not long after being joined a few rows down by the Rt. Hon. Kenneth Clarke, we were summarily evicted by an over-zealous official from the very nice seats we had chosen for the session after tea, and had to endure, oh, at least an hour and a half in the sun. Still, it was late afternoon sun, its sting already drawn.

Meanwhile, out in the middle, the puzzle of the Trent Bridge shirtfront remained. Two further batsmen reached 50 without getting to 100, making it eight so far in the match, and if you throw in another two who made it past 40 but only to 45, you begin to wonder whether this wicket isn't deliberately mocking all of us who have been going on so about its high-scoring reputation. The story of the day anyway, from my angle, can be summed up thus. During the first half of it Australia dispatched England economically enough, to gain a significant lead, one that should have enabled them completely to shut the home side out of the game by close of play. In the second half of the day, however, they failed to do this, even though they finished plainly having the upper hand. Three ill-chosen shots are responsible for their failure to lock the door.

The day began with Thorpe being dropped in the gully by Steve Waugh of all people, off the bowling of McGrath; not a sitter, but one you would have expected Waugh to take. Thorpe was on 31 at the time and he got to his half-century and, with Adam Hollioake, to the 100 partnership for the fifth wicket. But the damage was limited. On 243 both of them departed. Hollioake was brilliantly caught by Taylor off Reiffel for 45, Taylor diving to his right behind Mark Waugh who was diving to *his* left, obscuring Taylor's view. In the very next over from Warne, Thorpe was caught off his glove by Blewett at forward short leg, though the contact with the glove was hard to detect at a distance or from the replay, so causing some dismay amongst the crowd. In any event, Thorpe was out for 53, and Croft came and, surprisingly, didn't at once leave again. He struck some effective blows off Warne, including a six. But he went soon enough and in the way we have come to expect. Just before lunch, he fended a delivery from McGrath gently into Blewett's hands and the players trooped off with England on 272 for 7.

Ladbrokes time again for me. A fiver on England at 33 to 1. Not as good odds as at Headingley but better than at Old Trafford. 160-odd quid will do nicely if England were somehow to manage to level the series, and it would blast my debt to Ian out of the water. And if they don't manage it, who cares? The money, in that case, was to propitiate those inscrutable cricketing gods.

The England innings was wrapped up pretty swiftly after lunch. On 290 both Ben Hollioake and Andy Caddick were out, Hollioake caught by Mark Waugh at second slip off Reiffel, Caddick by Healy off McGrath. Devon Malcolm then did what, as a batsman, everyone always wants him to do, namely have a heave. He struck three fours, to the enormous pleasure of the crowd. This pleasure is, if anything, heightened by the ludicrousness of the defensive shots he essays in between these connecting blows, ungainly to the point, one might even imagine, of deliberate comedy. It was brief enjoyment. Malcolm was soon bowled, sort of jumping over a slower ball from McGrath, and England were all out for 313, giving Australia a lead of 114.

Ian, one run within getting the exact innings total, went yet a further £1 ahead of me and, by McGrath's two late dismissals, robbed me of the 50p I would otherwise have won for picking Shane Warne. Each bowler had taken four wickets, but McGrath for 71 and Warne for 86. There seems to be no bottom to the trough

I have fallen into with this side bet business, and I am developing a theory as to why it is. Ian just bets – ruthlessly – on what he estimates is likely to happen. I am regularly confused between what I think *might* happen, what I *want* to happen, and worries about the *effects* my bets could have one way or another on the cricket itself. So anxious, in fact, was I about all this at the start of the Australian second innings that I had to plead for an extra couple of minutes to settle my thoughts. The anxiety related chiefly to the possibility of Australia now messing things up with the Ashes so nearly in the bag.

I could have spared myself the worst anxieties at least; there was no calamity. The first two wickets realised just over 50 apiece, three of the top four Australian batsmen made it to scores in the middle range, so to say, and Australia got to 167 for 4 by the close – equivalent, with their lead, to 281 for 4. And yet only Mark Waugh didn't give his wicket away. Waugh never looked in, especially against Dean Headley, and he was soon lbw to him for 7. Elliott, Taylor and Blewett, on the other hand, were all well established and among the runs by the time they got themselves out hooking, or trying to, for (respectively) 37, 45 and 60. Elliott, it has to be said, was out to a stupendous catch by Crawley off Caddick on the square-leg boundary. His luck, so beneficent at both Lord's and Headingley, had run right out, for nine times out of ten the catch Crawley took would have been spilled if it had even gone to hand. Elliott lofted an enormous blow out in his direction and Crawley had to make some ground even to get his hands under it, the barest fraction from the turf. But, judging it to a nicety, he got there, clung on to the ball and held his arms aloft in triumph. All of his team mates raced out to him on the boundary and so they should have. Even in my disappointment I was delighted by the catch – and to have had such a good view of it – eclipsing, now, all other contenders for the best catch of the series so far: McGrath's to dismiss Butcher at Old Trafford, Mark Waugh's at Headingley, and Taylor's earlier during this same day.

After that, Taylor and Blewett took the score from 51 for 1 to 105 for 2, Taylor mis-hooking Ben Hollioake to give Hussain a very simple, lobbed catch half way to the boundary; and, another 50-odd runs on – Mark Waugh having departed in the meantime – Blewett, who had patiently put together an attractive 60, wafted feebly to a ball going down leg-side from Caddick and was caught behind. 156 for 4 and my anxiety level high. Steve Waugh and Ricky Ponting saw

Australia to stumps and remain there for the morning. What will happen? One can only wait and find out.

But the ugliest thing I have seen yet during this series was sitting a little way to the left of us after tea today. His face made red with the effort and whole body trembling with frustration and rage, he periodically abused Michael Atherton and the England players, offering them unfriendly information and advice: such as that the Ashes were at stake; and that they ought to work more as a team. Despite England's successes of the afternoon, it all evidently became too much for this poor man and he left half an hour before the close, I hope in order to seek psychiatric help.

Fourth Day

It's all over but for the Oval Test which now assumes a quite different level and kind of interest. Who could have thought, at the end of the third day, that the game would not make it into the fifth? In fact, Ian and I experienced our own little reversal of the Headingley 1981 situation, when the England team had booked out of their hotel on the penultimate morning, only to have to book back in after Botham had worked his famous transformation. We, by contrast, having initially booked our stay (at Nottingham Trent University) through to Saturday night in case the game should last only four days, requested an extension for Sunday night. Before the fourth day began, neither of us could believe that 16 wickets would fall in three sessions; not, surely, on this wicket and given what had gone before. But fall they did, the Ashes are safe with Australia and the first day at Edgbaston now seems to belong to another era.

Unyieldingly partisan in this affair as I am, and pleased also as I was by the morning session, I must confess to a feeling of how cruel a morning it was for the England camp. Having struck the very first ball of the day majestically to the boundary at cover point, Steve Waugh received a beast of a delivery from Caddick which he could only ward off to Adam Hollioake at second slip in order to protect his own person. Waugh, your main man, out second ball of the morning for 14 and Australia 171 for 5, their overall lead still manageable. It must have given hope. But before the hour was up, that hope was reduced to rubble as Ian Healy, with Ponting in a supporting role, took the game out of England's sight, playing an innings such as he periodically does – so often, it seems, when Australia most needs it. The partnership was worth 75 off 12 overs before noon, Healy's own 50 came in 49 balls, and he and Ponting raised the 100 put on between them in an hour and a half. It was a killer partnership, the decisive period of the day. Healy was out before lunch, caught by Stewart off Adam Hollioake for 63, and the *ninth* batsman to get to 50 in this match without going on to make a century. But one question had been settled. Henceforth England could only hope not to lose; barring something extraordinary they would not win. Lunch was taken at 278 for 6.

We went back over to the Press Box to look for Martin Johnson. He wasn't there but, through a confusion by the steward at the entrance, we got Christopher Martin-Jenkins instead and complimented him on his Test reports. On the way back to our seats – in circumstances I perhaps won't describe – I ran across a young guy from my country of origin, a Zimbabwean with a custom-made tee-shirt bearing the legend on the front, 'Rout of Africa', and on the back, 'England's Greatest Humiliation Ever'. We exchanged the usual sort of information about where we both came from in our common homeland, and I asked who he was supporting in this series. Australia – obviously. Hence the tee-shirt.

The rest of the Australian innings was a mere footnote, really, to the essential business done in the pre-lunch session, although it realised something reasonably substantial, as the Australian lower order makes a habit of doing: a further 58 runs. Ponting was the third batsman in this match to be out for 45, caught by Stewart off Adam Hollioake; Warne struck a huge six off Croft before being caught by Thorpe off the same bowler for 20; Gillespie was also caught by Thorpe, this time at slip and off Headley for 4; and Reiffel was out for a useful 22, caught by Ben Hollioake off Croft. Australia had made 336, leaving England with an all but impossible task to win, 451 runs.

The tensest thing, however, during this passage of play was not centre stage but on the sidelines. Ian and I had entered the most nail-biting period in the whole history of our side-betting during the series. Up to 330, the innings total was in his territory; after 331, it was in mine. He was as uptight as I have seen him in this matter, concerned to preserve his superior record, while I badly needed to restore my honour. And so I did, let it be, here, clearly marked. Not only was my estimate closer but, coming in within five of the actual total, I clawed back £1 of my ever-growing debt.

The England second innings, beginning at 3.00, is an abject tale. They were bowled out in just under 49 overs, playing not as if to save the game and at least keep the series open, but in order to stay ahead of the required run rate – or so it appeared – in the hope of working a miracle and pushing the Ashes to one further contest at the Oval. However, McGrath, Gillespie and Warne each claimed three wickets, Reiffel chipped in with one, and the arrivals and departures of England batsmen assumed something of the regularity of those airliners in the sky above the Lord's pavilion. The only partnership of any magnitude was one of 53 between Thorpe and Crawley, approached as though the two of them were in the final stretch of some unimportant limited overs game. Notable events within the dismal procession were that Thorpe survived for a score of 82 not out, preserving to the very end the 'no hundreds' law of this Trent Bridge Test; that, in a mirror image of Warne's departure to the bowling of Croft in the Australian innings, Croft here struck a six off Warne immediately before losing his wicket to him; and that Healy, diving in front of first slip to dismiss Headley off McGrath, took the third stunning catch of the game, following Taylor's and Crawley's. This was after the Australian captain, needing just two more wickets, had claimed the extra half-hour to save us from returning on the final morning. Malcolm then went with just seven balls to spare, England were out for 186, and Australia had won by 264 runs. After participating in the final rites beneath the pavilion, Ian and I headed for home.

For me there is nothing like it in all of sport, the winning of the Ashes. Explain it who can, but there beneath the pavilion, like some usurper to a prize not his own, I shared the joy of all Australia, cricketers and followers, as though a true native of that distant land. Australia, you beauty!

Having begun in such spirited fashion in early June, England ended up being overwhelmed before the middle of August, by a side gone from vulnerable to mighty again. An index of the extent of Australia's superiority, one I have not seen remarked upon, was that on what is universally acknowledged to have been the best batting pitch of the series, they bowled England out twice using only four bowlers. That two of these were Shane Warne and Glenn McGrath – arguably the greatest ever practitioner of the leg-spinner's art, and a fast bowler who looks destined, at the moment anyway, to find his place amongst the very best of that intimidating tradition – helps to explain this. Raking over the still warm Ashes, one can only concur with the view now being expressed by more than one of the pundits (Ian Chappell in the *Sunday Times*, Matthew Engel in the *Guardian* of the following morning) that this Australian team is one of the teams of all time. One could write of all 11 of them, not a weak link there after the dropping of Bevan and the recovery of Taylor. But let us consider just two, neither of these the most radiant stars with bat or ball. First Ian Healy, man of this match with seven catches and *the* innings here, Alec Stewart's notwithstanding. Behind the wicket, with bat in hand and in every way, Healy is the full set: toughest of competitors and one of the greatest of the wicket-keeping greats. Second, not one of the greats but, in a different mould, Paul Reiffel. A bowler of utmost reliability, rarely the destroyer of an innings but economical, consistent, usually the contributor of an important wicket or two; and, coming in number nine, someone who bats well enough for an average so far in this series of nearly 60. One, perhaps eccentric, way of putting the difference between Australia and England in the summer of 1997 is that the former had a player like Paul Reiffel, the latter, one like Mark Ealham.

When all is said and done, therefore – and grateful as I am to Jenny's stone, not to speak of all the other tokens of good fortune – Australia have won the Ashes yet again because they are a brilliant side, and the superstitions are as nothing. Well I never.

II

Thursday

In England during the run-up to the fifth Test the cricketing public settled to one of its favourite pastimes: debating the parlous state of the national game. Events at Headingley were certainly sufficient to trigger this debate, but as it happens a report by ECB chairman Lord MacLaurin on the structure of English cricket provided an alternative focus for it. In *Raising the Standard* MacLaurin argued that the County Championship should be turned into three American-style conferences with play-offs at the end of the season, that the Sunday League and Benson and Hedges Cup should be merged into a two-division, 50-over National League with promotion, relegation and, I guess, play-offs at the end of the season, that the NatWest Trophy should also be reduced to 50 overs and opened to 60 teams, that the second XI and minor counties championships should be turned into a 38-club championship, and that a national network of premier leagues should be created for club sides by 1999. MacLaurin's report was an ambitious attempt to change cricketing structures from top to bottom, with the aim of increasing competition throughout and promoting excellence. I found analyses of it hard to digest, commentators in the newspapers identified a number of incoherences, and the Trent Bridge Test – which England had to win on the basis of existing structures and resources to stand a chance of regaining the Ashes – slowly ticked around.

Meanwhile, in Sri Lanka on the eve of that Test some of the most important cricketing records in the book bit the dust. Responding in Colombo to India's first-innings 537 for 8 declared, Sri Lanka posted 952 for 6, thereby surpassing the record 903 for 7 declared set by England (against Australia) at the Oval in 1938. In the process, Sanath Jayasuriya and Roshan Mahanama put on 576 for the second wicket, a new record Test partnership, beating the 467 amassed for the third wicket by New Zealanders Andrew Jones and Martin Crowe (against Sri Lanka) in 1991. The one record that might have fallen but lived to fight another day was Brian Lara's individual score of 375, which Jayasuriya had in his sights until he was dismissed for 340 and returned to the pavilion in tears. The news that one of cricket's newest Test-playing nations was tearing up the record books provoked cynicism among some about the state of the Colombo wicket. Among others it prompted renewed introspection about the state of the English game.

The weather naturally maintained its place in the counsels of the nation, serving up sufficient rain in the days before the Test to flood parts of southern England (and whole swathes of continental Europe). 'Forget the drought: August gets back to normal' ran a front-page *Independent* headline on the first day of the fifth Test. Not so, however, at Trent Bridge, where the sun shone punishingly from a sky which was clear, blue and cloudless at the start and finish of the first day, with no more than the odd passing cloud glimpsed in between. Indeed, this was a day on which Norm and I scanned the skies in the hope of finding clouds that might provide some respite from the heat – it's strange how the parameters of skywatching can change – but we were certainly not so fickle as to forget that, for cricketing purposes at least, it is better to be roasted alive than drowned.

In the sunshine in which it was bathed when Norm and I arrived and walked to our seats in the Hound Road Stand (Lower), Trent Bridge looked superb. We had also admired it on a trip in 1995 to see the West Indies share a largely unmemorable day's cricket with England. Now we were happy to confirm its ranking as our favourite English Test ground outside London. For me it gained this status not for great architecture or an imposing pavilion, neither of which it has, but for sheer charm, notably on its western side where white stands flow round the ground. I said to Norm that this was how I imagined some of the great provincial grounds in Southern Africa to be (particularly on a day of massive heat). Not entirely, he replied, though on reflection he could see something in the comparison. Passing Ladbrokes, we poked our noses in to check the odds: Australia 5 to 4, England 7 to 1, the draw 4 to 5. 7 to 1 on England in a contest in which only three results were possible? It was almost insulting.

In the long interval before start of play – our arrival having been massively early – Norm and I discussed previous contests on this ground. Norm recalled that when, at the end of the 1989 Ashes series already won by Australia, Geoff Marsh and Mark Taylor batted the entire day for some 300 runs, one tabloid newspaper felt itself pushed beyond endurance. 'How much more can we take?' ran its headline the next day. That match was also Atherton's first for England (and Malcolm's). And now here was Atherton walking out with the self-same Mark Taylor – who had gone on to make a double century in 1989 – to hear the Australian captain call correctly for the fifth time in five in this series and announce that his team would bat. On a flat wicket in these conditions it cannot have been a difficult decision. Following their Headingley triumph, Australia were unchanged. England, by contrast, had dropped Butcher, Ealham and Smith – the first two being somewhat unfortunate to go – and had lost Gough to injury. In their place were Caddick and Malcolm, returning, and the Hollioake brothers, Adam and Ben, both making their debuts. They were the first brothers to play for England since the 1950s, and the first to be called up together since the nineteenth century. It would be an understatement to say that the nation had high hopes of them; 'Holli-mania' is how Martin

Johnson described it in the *Telegraph*. Ben had played a mere 12 first-class matches for Surrey prior to his international debut, and at 19 was one of England's youngest-ever players. We placed our side bets. Norm: Mark Waugh (for how long could this go on?), Malcolm, 352. Ian: Blewett, Headley, 452.

As with Atherton in 1989, day one of the fifth Test did not provide the ideal forum for the Hollioakes to strut their stuff. Taylor had been no mug in choosing to bat on a wicket on which even he looked largely untroubled. There was the odd scare in the opening passage of play – indeed, throughout the day English bowlers found an edge here and there – but on the whole the Australians had things entirely their way. 84 for 0 at lunch, 181 for 2 at tea, and 302 for 3 at the close tell their own story. Unusually, however, that story had no main protagonist. Instead, it was one of those days when no batsman fails and none dominates. A decent-sized half-century was par for the course: Elliott 69, Taylor 76 (taking him, at 61, past 6000 runs in Test cricket), Blewett 50 and Mark and Steve Waugh undefeated on 60 and 38 at the finish. On the second day, of course, either or both of the not out batsmen could easily score big hundreds. For England too there were no outstandingly good or bad performances. The three fast bowlers – Headley, Malcolm and Caddick – all performed well, with Caddick possibly the pick. The ball with which he bowled Taylor was a beauty. Croft was tidy and inexpensive without ever looking particularly menacing. Ben Hollioake went for 23 in his first three-over spell, but returned to pick up Blewett – caught Stewart – for his first Test wicket.

A superb start, then, for Australia, which Norm and I watched from a variety of seats in our efforts to evade the sun. The ones we had paid for in row F were shaded till 12.25. Thereafter we were chased ever deeper into the stand as the sun made its way across the heavens. By close of play we were thanking our lucky stars to be seated in a part of the ground awash with corporate hospitality, which made for easy pickings on the seat front at all times other than the 50 minutes or so before tea. Then we had to resort to hats, shades and, in Norm's case, a shirt over the head.

Friday

Norm and I settled to the second day of the Trent Bridge Test fully expecting great things of Australia. Norm was keen to see centuries by Mark Waugh, Steve Waugh, Ricky Ponting and any member of the Australian tail who cared to score one. Particularly, though, he hoped for Mark Waugh to make it to three figures, the rest of the Australian top six all having done so already at some point in the series. In the papers Mark Taylor was quoted as saying that 300 had been the target for the first day, and that the same again was the aim on the second. 'What, he actually *said* that?' Norm was already reading danger signals into this statement and fearing that the cricketing gods would punish Taylor for his hubris.

He turned out to be right: they did. As the morning session unfolded it became clear that the luck was now with England, at least to a greater extent than on the first day when their three fast bowlers had found a fair few edges only to see them fall short of fielders. Again it was those bowlers who did the damage, with Caddick, Headley and Malcolm all bowling excellent spells to reduce the Australians to 405 for 8 by lunch. Mark Waugh went first when, following two leg-side glances for four off Caddick, he was trapped lbw by the same bowler for 68. Ponting then became the first person to be dismissed for less than 50 in the match, falling to Headley for 9. Next Malcolm produced an excellent spell to dismiss Healy, Warne and Steve Waugh in the space of 20 deliveries. Of the three, only Waugh, with 75, had made any sort of score. 103 for 5, then, in the morning session: not at all what had seemed probable. Among the sweepstakers sitting next to us there was a 372 for 8 by lunch and a 403 for 3. We didn't know whether they had devised a rule to decide between these competing claims on the pot.

The strange aspect of the Australian innings, which Norm and I debated while munching our sandwiches, was the fact that all top five batsmen had got to 50, but none had gone on to 100. Four of the five were out between 68 and 76. Testimony, we thought, to the English bowlers' determination and stamina even when things did not look so great for them. The blame for Australia's comparative collapse on the second day was ascribed by Norm to Mark Taylor. Never tempt fate by making rash prophecies was the lesson.

I wondered what would happen after lunch. 'Presumably,' said Norm in his matter-of-fact voice, 'Australia will be all out for something between 405 and 420.' He rarely can judge these things: they made it to 427. Once again the side-bet victory for innings total was mine: at least the sixth or seventh in a row. Headley's success in claiming the last two wickets in the innings also gave me best bowler. The first of those wickets was Reiffel's – caught Thorpe for 26 – to bring his series average down to 78.5.

125 for 7 on the day was certainly a triumph for England, but there was still the small matter of the 302 for 3 notched up on the first day to contend with. And for some reason this flat batsman's wicket – 'a bland shirt front' (whatever that means) according to Pringle in the *Indie* – was giving undeniable help to fast bowlers. We made our England innings selections. Ian: Atherton (still loyal, despite a string of disappointments lately), Gillespie, 314. Norm: Ben Hollioake, Warne (in place of Gillespie, his first choice), 352.

What followed was immensely cheering for England supporters. Atherton and Stewart came out at 2.15 and put on an untroubled century partnership for the first wicket before Atherton was caught by Healy off Warne for 27 with the England score 106. It was a shame to see the captain go, but the real action was taking place at the other end, where Stewart was building a more commanding innings than any seen by an English – or even Australian – batsman in the entire series. In a single over from Gillespie – the fourteenth of the innings – Stewart hit four fours and a two to take the England score from 39 (three an over) to 57 (just above four an over). On a number of occasions he hit Warne to the boundary during a contest which was one of the keenest we had seen. Stewart's 50 came off 61 balls with 10 fours. He continued to dominate the Australian attack as he moved towards what looked like being a very well-deserved century. Then, on 87, disaster struck when he edged a ball from Warne and Healy knocked it up, swivelled, and just managed to get a glove under it as it fell behind him. The umpires consulted: had Healy actually taken the ball cleanly? Before they had completed their deliberations, however, Stewart walked and the ground rose to him. Even Norm was rather ashamed to have hexed Stewart on the Australian danger number. England 129 for 2.

This, it soon became clear, was the start of a middle-order collapse. Hussain was beautifully bowled for 2 by a delivery from Warne which pitched on middle and leg and hit off stump, in the process becoming the leg-spinner's third critical dismissal of the innings. 'Warne whammy', as the *Sun* was to put it next day, which is exactly what it was. Crawley went to a brilliant leg-side catch by Healy off McGrath for 18. England at this stage were 141 for 4, and the follow-on looked a real possibility. Indeed, had Thorpe been run out for 0, as he so very nearly was by a brilliant pick-up and throw from Gillespie which hit the wicket and prompted the adjudication of the third umpire, England would have been in real trouble. As it was, their innings moved temporarily into stasis, and the scoring rate which Stewart had left above four slipped towards three. It never quite made it there though, as towards the finish Thorpe and Adam Hollioake woke up to the fact that this was, after all, a batsman's wicket, and put together a few runs. England were looking a lot healthier on 188 for 4 at the close. With 313 runs scored and 11 wickets taken, the day bore some resemblance to epic days at Edgbaston and Headingley, though in truth this one had not had the concentrated drama of the first and third days of those Tests.

Again, the Trent Bridge Test had been played in sweltering conditions. It was possibly not quite as hot as the first day – said over the public address system to have been the hottest of the year – but it was still steaming at around 30 degrees. Norm and I replayed our shade-seeking routine, and were very fortunate to have to spend no more than 35 minutes of the afternoon session in our sun-drenched seats. Never again will I criticise corporate hospitality. It provides a lifeline for individuals who have 'just come for the cricket' (as Norm's neighbour at Headingley put it) by dragging others off to champagne receptions and freeing up their excellent seats.

By 10.00 in the evening Norm – bless him – had worked out a way in which England could still win the fifth Test and keep the Ashes contest alive: add a further 300 on the third day, bowl Australia out for 200 on the fourth, and score the 140 needed for victory on the fifth. He resolved to check Ladbrokes' odds on this the next morning.

Saturday

As the third day got under way it seemed that Australia might have lost some of the razor sharpness that had played such a major part in their success to this point in the series. In the fifth over of the first session – about the point at which on the previous day Caddick had trapped Mark Waugh lbw to set up England's five-wicket morning

– Thorpe flashed at McGrath outside off stump and saw Steve Waugh spill a difficult but, as these things go, by no means unmakeable catch. What would have been 191 for 5 remained for 4. Thorpe's 31 remained undefeated.

For a while it seemed an important miss. Thorpe and Adam Hollioake made good progress and even registered a century partnership. Then, however, the Australian machine rolled back into action, wickets started to tumble, and the English innings was wrapped up for 313 at around 2.20, just over 24 hours after it had been opened. The first dismissal of the day – Adam Hollioake for a good debut 45 – saw Taylor take a brilliant catch at first slip behind a diving Mark Waugh at second. This catch took Taylor's international tally to 122, level (from fewer Tests) with Greg Chappell and Viv Richards, and second only to Allan Border's 156. Indeed, as a specialist first slip who can bat a bit, Taylor is having a superb series. Only the dropped catch off Butcher in England's second innings at Lord's – admittedly a relatively easy and important chance – sticks in the memory. The second dismissal of the day – Thorpe out next over, caught Blewett bowled Warne for 53 – initially looked straightforward. A dolly catch had been readily snapped up by forward short leg. On the big screen replay, however, it became clear that no bat had been involved in the dismissal. Was it then lbw? A further replay showed that the line was clearly wrong for that. This left a glove-pad catch as the only alternative to the worst decision of the series. Next day none of the papers made much fuss about it, so some glove must have been involved. England had moved from 243 for 4 to 243 for 6.

Meanwhile, Ben Hollioake was looking positive and effective: 13 runs came off one Reiffel over. But in the next Reiffel showed that he is not a man to be pushed around by some teenage upstart, having Hollioake caught by Mark Waugh in the slips for 28. Croft, disappointingly, gave Blewett one of the easiest catches of the series off McGrath to go for 18. What should have been the penultimate ball before lunch became the ultimate. Norm pottered off to put £5 on an England victory at 33 to 1.

That just left fun and games for the afternoon session, provided chiefly by Devon Malcolm: fairly assured on the attack, decidedly not so on the defensive. It also settled important side-bet issues between Norm and me. By taking the final two wickets of the innings, McGrath finished with a marginally better analysis than

Warne, and thereby deprived Norm of 50p. By nudging the total up to 313 with a partnership of 23 for the tenth wicket, Headley and Malcolm took it to within one run of my prediction: £1 for me, and an extension of my inexplicable run of success. Australia 114 runs ahead, then, their fourth consecutive lead on first innings (and every one of them significant). Side bet time again. Norm: Elliott, Headley, 340. Ian: Mark Waugh (it was just possible he would choose this innings to shine), Caddick, 321.

As usual, Elliott came out full of bluster: 37 runs out of 51. Then, however, he was out to a blinder of a catch by Crawley taken at full stretch, an inch or two off the turf and just in from the boundary rope. It was so good that it seemed almost inconceivable that Crawley had made it. Next Taylor and Blewett put together a further 50 partnership before each chose to gift his wicket to England by mistiming a hook. Taylor went for 45 (and 121 in the match), Blewett for 60 (and 110 in the match). In between, Mark Waugh, who at no point looked settled, fell lbw to Headley for 7. Through all of this Norm was his normal anxious self. When Waugh went, he pronounced the game to be 'uncomfortably close'. The effective Australian score at the time was 248 for 3. If a fifth wicket had gone down before the finish he would have considered England to be back in the hunt. Well it didn't, and by the close Australia were so far ahead – 281 runs – as to be almost out of sight.

There was an odd aspect to the day. Its first session saw 84 runs added, precisely the same number as during the first session of the first day. Similarly, its second session saw 97 runs added, again the exact amount scored during the second session of the first day. In the third session the parallel broke down: 121 runs on the first day, 111 on the third. There was, however, a further echo of the recent past. On the third day, as on the second, 125 runs were added to the overnight first innings total before the tenth wicket fell. These sorts of things have been going on all series, but neither Norm nor I has felt it right to report them.

Again the sun shone mercilessly all day long. We succeeded in spending the entire afternoon session in the shaded corporate block. After tea, however, just when we were congratulating ourselves on sitting a mere four rows behind Kenneth Clarke MP – 'What, the real one?' asked Norm, past master of fake celebrity sightings – an officious steward turned up to clear us back to our proper seats and two hours (for me) of sitting with shirt draped over head.

This cover was, however, not sufficient to block out the angry shouted comments of one of the most agitated characters I have ever seen at the cricket (or anywhere else), or indeed the remarks of the lumpen bourgeoisie in the corporate hospitality seats which were at least as offensive as anything emanating from the remarkably quiescent Barmy Army at the Radcliffe Road End of the ground. Norm, driven to distraction by chants throughout the series of 'Stand up if you hate Man U', actually joined the corporates in a lusty chorus of 'Ooh ah, Eric Cantona'. 'These are my friends', he insisted, beaming. When Mr Angry could take no more and left before close of play, one of the corporate wags finally came out with a funny remark. 'Bye. Hope you've had a nice day!'

Sunday

The two directions in which the fourth day of the Trent Bridge Test could go were dramatically illustrated by the first two deliveries of the morning. Steve Waugh struck the first ball of Caddick's over for a handsome four. Off the second, a superb lifting delivery, he was caught by Adam Hollioake at second slip for 14. The fifth Test seemed set to remain competitive to the last.

However, as has been the way of things in this series, that impression was quickly corrected by Australia. In what can only be described as a devastating display of strokeplay, Healy in particular and Ponting to a lesser extent took the game to England to such a degree that at the end of 12 overs from Caddick, Headley and Malcolm, Australia had added 75 runs for the loss of Waugh's wicket. The introduction of Croft slowed things down considerably, with the result that in the remaining 17 overs of the morning session Australia added only 36 runs. They also lost Healy – caught Stewart bowled Adam Hollioake – for an excellent 63 struck off 78 balls. But it was undeniably Australia's morning.

For England there was the renewed frustration of watching Stewart miss an easy stumping chance, as at Headingley given by Ponting off Croft. At Headingley Ponting had been on 109 when the chance went begging. Here he was on 40, and the Australians were 277 for 6. They lost no more wickets before lunch, taken one run later. A lead of 392 surely put them out of reach. At Ladbrokes odds on an England victory of 20 to 1 at start of play had been lengthened to 100 to 1.

In the afternoon session each of Norm's latest targets was met as leads of 400, 427 (the Australian first innings total) and 450 were posted. Slowly, too, Australian wickets fell. Again Ponting failed to make much of Stewart's failure to stump him, being out for 45 to the combination that had seen off Healy. Very late in the day Croft finally had Warne and Reiffel caught to bring him match figures of 2 for 117. Reiffel, who certainly would have been run out had Stewart gathered a good throw from the boundary cleanly, made even less of his good fortune than had Ponting. Next ball he was caught by Ben Hollioake off Croft for 22 to reduce his series average still further to 59.67. The Australian innings came to an end on 336. Not only had a final flourish from the tail taken the total beyond my 321 and within range of Norm's 340, it had also placed it sufficiently close to win him £1. At least the split of tail-end wickets between Croft and Headley left Caddick with the best analysis – 3 for 85 – and enabled me to recoup 50p for that. England had been set 451 in 132 overs to win. We placed side bets – Ian: Atherton, Warne, 279; Norm: Hussain, McGrath, 300 – before being moved from our adopted seats in the shade to our proper ones in the sun.

England's reply looked secure enough until the fourth ball of the ninth over – also the final over before tea – when Atherton was once again trapped by a rising delivery from McGrath and caught by Healy for 8. Remarkably, this was the sixth time out of nine dismissals in the series that Atherton had fallen to McGrath. England 25 for 1 at tea. That soon became 25 for 2 when Reiffel had Stewart caught by Steve Waugh for 16 off the first ball of the tenth over. Still all was not lost, for Crawley and Hussain put together a 50 partnership at four an over before Hussain was bowled by Gillespie for 21. At this point, however, the collapse began in earnest as Gillespie, in an extraordinary spell of 8 overs, took 3 for 65 to tear out England's middle order. For the second time in the match Crawley was caught behind down the leg-side, this time for a good-looking 33. It was hard to figure out what was going on out there. Were England actually going for victory, the sole result that would keep open the possibility of winning the Ashes? It was the only plausible explanation for their excessively cavalier approach.

Norm and I watched the start of the day's final session in the shade among the VIPs. It was one of the most unpleasant sections of crowd we had experienced all series. To our right was a loud-mouthed and obnoxious know-it-all who had clearly taken a great fancy both to himself and to some of the surrounding company. 'I like women that's got *no* scruples!' To our left were purveyors of racist jokes. As background mood music to all this was a series of mainly anti-Warne songs (some of which Warne himself – Fatboy to most crowds – took to conducting from third slip) from the Barmy Army's small Radcliffe Road End stand.

As ever, Warne had the final word, taking the wickets of Ben Hollioake and Caddick lbw – rarities in themselves – and that of Croft caught McGrath the delivery after Croft had struck a six. At 6.30, with England 173 for 8, Taylor claimed the extra half-hour, and a minimum of eight overs. With the third ball of the seventh of those overs McGrath had Headley superbly caught by Healy in front of Taylor at first slip for 4. With the fifth ball he had Malcolm caught by Mark Waugh for 0. England 186 all out – with Thorpe undefeated on 82 at the close – meant that Australia had won the match by 264 runs and the series 3-1 (with one to play). They would have won here by the Old Trafford margin of 268 runs had they not conceded four wholly unnecessary overthrows at the very end of the day's play. It was an equally stunning victory. As the champagne flowed Tony Greig selected Ian Healy as man of the match, correctly noting that he had scarcely made a mistake all series. Norm and I calculated that I was now £3.50 ahead in side bets.

This was in many ways an outstanding day in an excellent series. 355 runs for 16 wickets in 95.4 overs were all series records. The day's main significance was, of course, its reinforcement of Australian dominance, which now stood at somewhere near total. Since their defeat in the first Test the Australians had rarely looked troubled, even though they had sometimes been thought to be so. As late as 3 July, the first morning of the third Test at Old Trafford, Pringle had written in the *Independent* that 'the Australians may feel – with England carefully nursing a one-match lead – that the Ashes are slowly slipping away'. Not quite. Their grip on the Ashes was now as tight as ever and their superiority in all departments – batting, bowling, fielding – was clear. Thinking after the match about selections for a best XI from the players who had appeared in the series to date, it seemed likely that only Hussain (for Mark Waugh) and possibly Thorpe (for Blewett) could dislodge anyone from the Australian team that had won at Headingley and Trent Bridge.

Looking to the future, it was hard to see what lessons England could draw from defeat. Some were positive. The Hollioakes had not performed miracles, but they had made assured and useful debuts and were clearly here to stay. More were negative, with many, inevitably, focusing on Atherton's captaincy. Saturday's *Sun* had actually run an 'Athers offers to quit' story. Although this was fiercely denied by both Lord's and Atherton himself, following such a decisive series defeat the speculation in the papers had to have some foundation. 'Atherton on brink', as the *Mail on Sunday* put it. I guess he will (have to) go, and very possibly it is right that he does so. It remains the case that England in this series have not been a bad cricketing side. Yet they are undeniably streets away from matching Australia. What to do about this is no easy matter.

On the road back to Manchester, Norm and I stopped for a pint. I asked the barman whether Spurs had beaten United at White Hart Lane in their opening Premiership clash of the season. Yes, they had! But in the detail he asked someone else to provide came the truth: 2-0 to United (despite a penalty miss by Tottenham reject Teddy Sheringham). It was a fitting end to the day.

Sixth Test
The Oval
21-23 August

Scorecard

England

M A Butcher b McGrath	5	lbw b M E Waugh	13
*M A Atherton c Healy b McGrath	8	c S R Waugh b Kasprowicz	8
†A J Stewart lbw b McGrath	36	lbw b Kasprowicz	3
N Hussain c Elliott b McGrath	35	c Elliott b Warne	2
G P Thorpe b McGrath	27	c Taylor b Kasprowicz	62
M R Ramprakash c Blewett b McGrath	4	st Healy b Warne	48
A J Hollioake b Warne	0	lbw b Kasprowicz	4
A R Caddick not out	26	not out	0
P J Martin b McGrath	20	c & b Kasprowicz	3
P C R Tufnell c Blewett b Warne	1	c Healy b Kasprowicz	0
D E Malcolm lbw b Kasprowicz	0	b Kasprowicz	0
Extras (b 2, lb 6, nb 10)	18	(b 6, lb 10, nb 4)	20
Total (56.4 overs)	180	(66.5 overs)	163

Fall of wickets 18, 24, 97, 128, 131, 132, 132, 158, 175

20, 24, 26, 52, 131, 138, 160, 163, 163

Bowling *First Innings* McGrath 21-4-76-7; Kasprowicz 11.4-2-56-1; Warne 17-8-32-2; Young 7-3-8-0 *Second Innings* McGrath 17-5-33-0; Kasprowicz 15.5-5-36-7; Warne 26-9-57-2; M E Waugh 7-3-16-1; Young 1-0-5-0

Australia

M T G Elliott b Tufnell	12	(2)	lbw b Malcolm	4
*M A Taylor c Hollioake b Tufnell	38	(1)	lbw b Caddick	18
G S Blewett c Stewart b Tufnell	47		c Stewart b Caddick	19
M E Waugh c Butcher b Tufnell	19		c Hussain b Tufnell	1
S R Waugh lbw b Caddick	22		c Thorpe b Caddick	6
R T Ponting c Hussain b Tufnell	40		lbw b Tufnell	20
†I A Healy c Stewart b Tufnell	2		c & b Caddick	14
S Young c Stewart b Tufnell	0		not out	4
S K Warne b Caddick	30		c Martin b Tufnell	3
M S Kasprowicz lbw b Caddick	0		c Hollioake b Caddick	4
G D McGrath not out	1		c Thorpe b Tufnell	1
Extras (lb 3, w 1, nb 5)	9		(b 3, lb 4, w 1, nb 2)	10
Total (79.3 overs)	220		(32.1 overs)	104

Fall of wickets 49, 54, 94, 140, 150, 164, 164, 205, 205

5, 36, 42, 49, 54, 88, 92, 95, 99

Bowling *First Innings* Malcolm 11-2-37-0; Martin 15-5-38-0; Caddick 19-4-76-3; Tufnell 34.3-16-66-7 *Second Innings* Malcolm 3-0-15-1; Martin 4-0-13-0; Tufnell 13.1-6-27-4; Caddick 12-2-42-5

England won by 19 runs
Umpires P Willey and L H Barker
Toss England

Splits

		Lunch	Tea	Close
First day	England	97-2	180	
	Australia			77-2
Second day	Australia	125-3	190-7	220
	England			52-3
Third day	England	145-6	163	
	Australia		50-4	104

I

Eve of Test

On my mind as I take the train to Euston are various cricketing matters. One is that, with the winning of the series, Australia's recent superiority over England has reached a new level. It is the first time this century that either of the two sides has been victorious in five consecutive Ashes series. Second, and whether or not connected with this, there are the continuing oddities of England's selection policy. It seems that through every turnover of selectorial regime a certain amount of pointless chopping and changing survives. Already there has been the misguided Smith-for-Caddick move at Headingley. Now, for the coming Test, Butcher returns and Crawley is dropped; Crawley who made 83 at Old Trafford in the only England second innings resistance to speak of there, and then 72 at Headingley, contributing by this to the most spirited English partnership of the match. The reason for the change, according to the *Guardian*'s correspondent, is that the experiment of having Stewart open the innings at Trent Bridge hadn't worked. Hadn't worked? Stewart made 87 in the first innings, in a display of batting dominance his team could use a lot more of. But no, it hadn't worked, you see, because Stewart had had to open both innings of the Nottingham Test after a long stint keeping wicket. The English selectors, then, are familiarising themselves with the way a two-innings cricket match can unfold, given the principle of an uncertain toss.

Third, standing on Piccadilly Station this morning and looking at a copy of *The Cricketer* in the station bookshop, I was delighted to read a piece by Martin Johnson lamenting the behaviour of the Barmy Army at Edgbaston and more generally. Hooray. Let all men and women of good will speak out. Take back the cricket grounds. Fourth, I was also pleased to note in *Wisden Cricket Monthly* that someone other than myself had seen fit to record the many scores of 1 there were in the Lord's Test. What this unnamed someone said, in fact, was the following: 'England's 77 was their lowest Test total ever not to include a duck. And they may well have set another record – the most batsmen out for 1 in one innings.' There are people who look into this kind of thing! What is it about cricket that encourages it? Well then, did anyone else notice that at Old Trafford the lunch-time score on both the first and the third days was the same, Australia 78 for 3? And has this ever happened before on two days of a Test match? On those two days or on any two days? I am reminded of an article I read (in *The Cricketer* of October 1989) by one Sam Garonner. This poor fellow had gone to the trouble of finding out what days of the week the best 100 or so post-war cricketers were born on, and of then picking teams for the different days. It seems from his researches that it may be good to have four people in your national side who were born on a Thursday.

I could go on some more like this but I had better stop. Otherwise I might get to remarking on the style of TV commentary of Mr Tony Lewis, whose 'ohs' and 'oohs' and other gasping exclamations, whether at a dismissal, close shave or even moderately testing delivery, put one in mind of an excitable young boy at his very first game. My co-author may well not approve of such end-of-series levity, not to say cheek, not to say prolixity before a single ball of the match has been bowled. To business therefore.

I travel to London much looking forward to this last Test. Though the outcome of the larger drama is no longer in doubt, which might be thought to detract from the interest of its final act, for me there are compensations. One is that I am now freed of anxiety. Naturally, I would prefer Australia not to lose this game, but even if they do that is all they will have lost. A 3-2 scoreline will make the series look closer than it really was and England would regain some pride, but I would not begrudge either point. Such a conclusion to the series may be thought unlikely in view of what has happened in the last three games. Speaking to England supporters, now sunk in deepest pessimism, that is the common reaction. However, the loss of Gillespie through injury, and Reiffel who has returned home because of complications in his wife's pregnancy, may weaken Australia somewhat. And it is not all that unusual for a team, with a series conclusively won, to lose the final match of it. I can think off-hand of 1966, 1974-75 and 1993. There, margins of 3-0, 4-0 and 4-0 to West Indies and Australia (twice) were narrowed by a victory for England at the death.

More important to my looking forward to the concluding Test of the series is something else, in any case, than freedom from anxiety. It is the venue: a ground I have never yet been to, though like anyone who follows cricket I know something about it. The Oval. The Oval for me is sun-drenched twilight: sun-drenched, because that is how the ground so often seems to be in late August; and twilight, because twilight is usually how it feels, another summer's contest slipping away, into shadow, towards memory. Or perhaps it might be that one particular summer has helped to fasten this dual image of the Oval in my mind: 1976, when great last events were played out on a field of parched brown, more Karachi than Kennington. The Oval has been the scene of so many great days and feats, familiar even to those who were not there to see them. 1948 and Bradman, in his final innings, bowled second ball for 0. 1953, when England recaptured the Ashes after a gap of more than 18 years. 1968 and Derek Underwood, after the deluge, bowling England to victory in the last half hour of the final day, to level a series in which Australia nevertheless kept the Ashes. Then 1976, Viv Richards's 291 and Michael Holding's stunning 14 wickets in the match on a flat pitch. And 1987, Javed Miandad's 260 in a Pakistan total of 708. So it goes on. I feel as if I have always known the place since I began to follow cricket. I have seen that gasholder, now, how many times. In fact, I have never seen it. Tomorrow I will.

First Day

For a first-time visitor to the Oval one immediate impression is of its size. As I walked around from the entrance nearest the underground station to our seats in the Gover Stand I already felt it, the dimensions here a different story from those of the other Test grounds. Then there are the names of Surrey and England on the way round. The Laker Stand and, next to it, the Lock; the Peter May Enclosure; the Jardine and Fender Stands; the Gover. Names of the all-conquering Surrey of my youth and before that. I wondered why May should enjoy the privilege of the 'Peter' but it seemed somehow fitting for the well-mannered sort of gent I imagine he was. Having arrived at the ground uncharacteristically early even for me, I took the opportunity of buying a couple of Ashes tee-shirts and a signed copy of the autobiography of David Boon – *Under the Southern Cross* – before settling in my seat.

The Oval from the Vauxhall End is a sight to behold. There is a grandeur about the pavilion, attached to the adjacent stands on both sides which are to it like two great outstretched arms embracing the field of play. Our seats, on the other hand, were not of the best. To say we were on a level with the wicket might be an exaggeration. With the slope of the ground away from the central square, it could be that our eyes were level with it, our lower bodies falling away. Still, we soon became accustomed to this new perspective. As Ian arrived, it had just been announced that Atherton – remarkably – had won the toss and chosen to bat. Big England score in prospect then. So we both thought, judging from our side bets. Ian took 442, and I, exploiting the huge swathe of possible scores underneath that, 420. They seemed reasonable sorts of estimate at the time, but they turned out wrong by a mile.

What we saw was another day of wickets tumbling, as though an extension of the Sunday at Trent Bridge. This was part of an awful England batting failure, and though two Australian wickets later gave them hope that the game would not immediately run right away, they certainly didn't get the best advantage from winning the toss. It started badly, with McGrath claiming the wickets of both openers, Butcher playing on trying to pull, for 5, Atherton getting an inside edge to Healy, for 8. But Stewart and Hussain took England from a dismal 24 for 2 to 97 by lunch, so that the poor start looked as if it might be down to early nerves or early life in the wicket and, either way, now left behind.

Not so. What happened after lunch was the traditional England-style plummet to disaster without qualification. Stewart was out lbw to the first ball he received after lunch; Hussain offered a low catch, taken by Elliott diving forward at mid-on; and Thorpe was bowled by a ball of superlative trajectory that snuck behind his legs to hit leg stump. All three of these wickets were also to McGrath, giving him five out of five so far. Warne then got into the act for variety, and variety is what it was, making a bit of a chump of Adam Hollioake who left alone what turned out to be a straight ball that bowled him. When Ramprakash, returning for what many well-wishers (including me) hoped would be a good, fresh beginning to his Test career, tamely spooned up a bat-pad catch off McGrath to Blewett at short leg, England were 132 for 7. They had lost five wickets since lunch for 35, the last four of them in the space of only four runs.

A short entertaining interlude followed. Caddick pulled a six over mid-wicket off Warne and Martin another to long leg off McGrath, for which McGrath treated him to a dose of the verbals, prompting Martin to stick out his tongue in response. For such temerity Martin was bowled next ball. Tufnell and Malcolm were then dispatched in their turn, caught by Blewett off Warne for 1 and lbw first ball to Kasprowicz for 0, and England were out for 180 just on the point of tea.

Without qualification a disaster. All one can say – repeat – is that it was by a great fast bowler that England were dismantled today. McGrath's performance, yielding him 7 for 76, was one of unrelenting hostility and intelligence, and it ranks with the 8 for 38 he took at Lord's with more help from the pitch there. He now has 36 wickets from the series, approaching, amongst Australians, Alderman's 42 in 1981 and 41 in 1989, Hogg's 41 in 1978-79 and Lillee's 39 in 1981; and this haul takes him past 150 wickets in Tests. But, disaster out in the middle notwithstanding, it was a bird of a different feather at the Vauxhall End: an unprecedented triumph in the side-betting department. Not only had I recovered from £3.50 to a mere £1.50 down (erasing more than half my debt at a stroke), I had achieved this by doing what neither of us had managed throughout the series, winning all three bets on the innings, and securing thereby an extra 50p bonus. Following my other, still unrepeated, first from Headingley – getting top batsman and top bowler in the same innings – I think I am making up in quality for Ian's vulgar quantity.

Australia begin their innings and for a while it looks bad for England. Though Elliott is unusually restrained, Mark Taylor is in threateningly good form. He hits three fours off a Malcolm over and another two off Martin's next. In no time Australia are 49 for 0. But then Tufnell, sent home all summer from the Test grounds of the land, is brought on to bowl and he at once puts obstruction in the way of the potential juggernaut. Tempting Elliott into an attacking shot, he spins the ball past his bat and bowls him. Taylor likewise tries to strike out and is caught by Hollioake on the reflex at forward short leg. The Australian openers have made 12 and 38 and Tufnell has 2 for 0. Blewett and Mark Waugh see Australia to the close on 77 for 2 with the help of some thin drizzle and bad light costing us nine overs.

Walking round the ground back towards the tube, Ian and I come upon a gang of autograph hunters by the players' entrance and we stop to look. We see most of the Australians – Healy, Warne, the Waughs, Taylor, others – as well as Thorpe, Gooch, Boycott and Peter Willey, one of this game's two umpires and as tough a nut in that role as he was as a player. Walking out of the ground, we again see Geoffrey Boycott, enquiring of someone at a bus stop whether he can get a bus from there to town. On the underground we read on the back of someone's *Evening Standard* its judgement of the day: 'Just humiliating', the headline shouts.

Second Day

As the last of six, the Oval Test is in mischievous end-of-term mood. Like Martin at McGrath, it has stuck out its tongue, and then pulled a face and flashed a cheeky grin. If the Trent Bridge wicket mocked us by allowing none of the many batsmen making 50 there to reach a century, the Oval, not to be outdone, has refused so far to deliver up even a single half-century. At the scene of Hutton's 364, Viv Richards's 291, Javed's 260 and more of that ilk, we have watched 23 wickets fall in less than two full days' play, each of them realising on average just under 20 runs. Not only that. One catch today was completed by the English wicket-keeper taking, and then firmly holding, the ball between his thighs. A front-line England batsman was dismissed by that front-line Australian bowler, Mark Waugh. Affected by the frivolous spirit at large in the neighbourhood, two otherwise reasonably serious people spent some time discussing this; that in moving towards a total of 218, Australia's score had at some point been at rest on all six of England's lower all-out totals of the series: on the 77 of Lord's, the 162 of Old Trafford, the 172 of Headingley, the 180 of the Oval itself, the 186 of Trent Bridge, and the 200 of Old Trafford, second innings. It must be time for everyone to go home. And if things carry on in the same way, it won't be long now before we do.

Early in the day there was some light rain and we lost most of the first hour to it. But there was a silver lining for Ian and me in that we massively improved our viewing position. Taking shelter in the Fender Stand and thereby escaping an insufferable chatterer behind us in the Gover, we were lucky to find seats, in a line behind the slips, that were unoccupied. Good old PGH. The day went, like yesterday, to the bowlers, in this case particularly Phil Tufnell, could it be making its own face at the England selectors? Mark Waugh was out before lunch to him, caught at silly mid-off by Butcher for 19. Then shortly after lunch, Steve Waugh, having played one or two of his 'no man move' shots to the off-side boundary, was lbw to

Caddick for 22, and 10 runs later Blewett was caught by Stewart for a top score in the match so far of 45, trying to sweep Tufnell to leg. Despite a couple of attractive fours, the batsman had struggled all through his innings to play a firm and secure stroke, and so his final tally was a credit to him in its way, testifying to his perseverance. However, 'Blewett caught Stewart' was a semi-rhyme I had not before noticed and I decided to look into it. Amazingly, having failed to occur in any of the first three Tests, it had occurred on every possible occasion since; as if, once the link had been established, it was unbreakable. Blewett, beware Stewart in the second innings!

By now, with the score 148 for 5, it was clear to us beyond room for further doubt that this was, contrary to expectation and Geoffrey Boycott (on the first evening's highlights), a bowlers' wicket. There was a period between lunch and tea, with Tufnell and Caddick, then Martin, in operation, when the runs nearly dried up altogether. The bowling was probing, persistent, tight. The English ground-fielding supported it nearly to a man, nearly because there is always Devon Malcolm; two stops, by Hussain and Atherton, were blinders.

Ponting became the rock – well, the rather large pebble anyway – of the latter part of the Australian innings, sticking around, accumulating, trying to achieve some stability. But the wickets continued to go down. Healy, even he unusually hemmed in while he lasted, his normal aggression stopped up, was taken off Tufnell by Stewart in that catch between the thighs, and Young was disposed of by the same combination but more conventionally. This made it 188 for 7 at tea. After which Warne, as is his way, gave us another breezy knock – this time of 30, including one giant straight six off Tufnell – before playing on to Caddick. The latter then immediately trapped Kasprowicz lbw, though lbw, it may be, on the bottom of his bat. It set up a possible hat-trick, but the hat-trick ball to McGrath passed harmlessly by him. Ponting was last out, caught by Hussain at slip off Tufnell, which gave Tufnell figures of 7 for 64. It was an admirable achievement. He had bowled an unbroken spell of 34.3 overs, nearly half of them maidens, and the pressure on the Australian batsmen was never lifted or relaxed. He just plugged away, levered them out one by one and bowled England back into a game everyone thought they must have forfeited.

Australia now had only a modest lead, but my, didn't they make the best of it. Any thought that England might quickly knock off these runs to begin to put themselves in significant credit was soon dispelled, as the pattern laid down in the match so far continued. Tight bowling, regular fall of wickets. The only surprise was that these went not to Warne or McGrath but to Kasprowicz and Mark Waugh, Waugh brought on late in the day to keep play going in light now become very dim. Atherton was out a second time for 8, caught in the gully by Steve Waugh off Kasprowicz. 20 for 1. Stewart was lbw for 3 to the same bowler. 24 for 2. Butcher was lbw to Mark Waugh – a decision that 'bordered on the scandalous' according to the even-handed Selvey – for 13. 26 for 3. Or minus 12 for 3. Deck-of-the-Titanic time once more. England at this point, like Australia before them earlier in the day, became seriously becalmed. In such dire peril Hussain and Thorpe played with all the care they could muster. But they kept the ship from crashing against the ice and, with a couple of boundaries then coming off Waugh, Mark Taylor evidently decided that the moment of greatest psychological pressure had passed for the day. He summoned Glenn McGrath as if to bring him back on and the umpires took everyone off for what was left of the day.

It is anybody's game. However, will it last till Sunday?

Third Day

No it didn't. The sort of thing I'd been fearing throughout the series, a recurrence of that Australian brittleness seen on the first morning at Edgbaston, finally came to pass, but only after it no longer mattered from the point of view of the overall result. So both Australia and England finished as they started, and I cannot think of another Test series quite like this – though in the long history of the game there probably is one – where the winning side is defeated first and last but puts together its necessary clutch of victories between the two sandwiching defeats. In any event, the series has finished with a cracking good contest and an exciting final day, and though my team lost I can't complain. It was fought by both sides down to the wire and deservedly won by England who used to their benefit that crucial resource, the burgeoning seed of doubt in a situation of pressure. This view is Matthew Engel's and seems appropriate: 'England took 10 [wickets] yesterday, getting such luck as was available from marginal umpiring decisions but deserving it for bowling and fielding like tigers and looking like a quality cricket team.' It appeared in the *Guardian* the day after the Oval Test – the Oval Test, that is, of 1993, when England also won a closing victory in a series already lost.

The day began pretty well for Australia. Hussain had a go at Warne's third ball of the morning and sliced a catch, nicely taken, to Elliott at short third man. Furthermore, in line with the nose-tweaking spirit of this Oval affair, overnight the Australian total had been revised upwards to 220 – and with it Blewett's score to 47 and Tufnell's analysis to 7 for 66 – as we were told by a very nice bloke from Belfast with whom we shared much conversation on this final day. From the TV evidence the third umpire had adjudged a four of yesterday to have been, really, a six. Imagine the reverse. A six becomes a four and a team that supposedly reached its winning target with the shot and then went home... what? Strange goings-on. There will be some discrepancies between the final scorecard and Ian's and my accounts of the second day.

Thorpe and Ramprakash now shared a crucial partnership of 79, playing as if they had realised or been instructed that just fiddling about was no longer to the point; on this wicket, where patient, accurate bowling would sooner or later yield a profitable harvest of fallen batsmen, runs expeditiously on the board were the thing. So the two of them pushed the score along and the runs they both made – Thorpe 62, sole half-century of the match, Ramprakash 48 – turned out to be crucial. Without these there was no England innings to speak of. One of the pair fell each side of lunch. Thorpe was caught off Kasprowicz by Taylor, another of this fine slip fielder's specials. The ball was passing him at speed and he latched on to it in the blink of an eye. Ian and I surmised that Taylor must have taken 10 catches in the series, but checking our scorecards we found it was only six, no more than one per Test. The quality of Taylor's catches perhaps accounts for this inflation of their number in both our minds. Ramprakash, just short of a good 50, was stumped by Healy off Warne, dancing down the track and missing the ball. Warne was now visibly limping, as I had not earlier noticed. Other than the partnership of Thorpe and Ramprakash, the England innings just folded up and all that need be further noted about it is that Healy took another of *his* fine catches, diving in front of first slip to dismiss Tufnell, and Kasprowicz finished with figures better than either McGrath's or Tufnell's: 7 for 36 to their 7 for 76 and 7 for 66.

Well, everyone now reckoned Australia must have it, with only 124 needed to win. Ian reckoned it, our friend from Belfast did, others sitting in the row behind us glumly did and even I sort of did. I mean, thought about cold sober – and this may be the point to record that, surrounded by great cohorts of drinkers, Ian and I consumed no alcohol in 26 days spent on the Test grounds of England; not through any general principle of abstemiousness, but just so, by cricket-watching preference – you obviously had to reckon that this Australian side, this Australian side now, would do it. There it was, the victory, beckoning, from not far beyond the 100 mark. All the same, and despite thinking earlier that their retention of the Ashes had delivered me from anxiety, I found I was very tense. For I could not bring myself to want anything else but an Australian victory and anyone who knows cricket knows that cold sober is one thing, but then there is also the stuff of dreams and nightmares, whirlpools, monsters. Of course Australia could lose. Because they did.

They lasted a mere 32.1 overs, two balls more than at Edgbaston, for a total of 104, and thus lost by the slim margin of 19 runs. No batsman made more than 20 (Ponting), only two partnerships realised double-figure amounts (31 between Taylor and Blewett, 34 between Ponting and Healy), and by the end the average yield for each wicket in this match had fallen below 17. With every wicket that went down the crowd became more febrile, expecting another dismissal on each delivery, willing another dismissal, seeing it even where there was no trace or suggestion of one. But the wickets kept on coming and Caddick and Tufnell shared them, 5 for 42 and 4 for 27 respectively. In so far as it is possible to identify key moments within a headlong rush to destruction, one here may have been the dismissal of Blewett, given out – caught Stewart! – when it is doubtful he touched the ball and looking as comfortable as any batsman in this innings. Another may have been the demise of Healy, always dangerous and beginning to score more freely after a faltering start. He gave a return catch which Caddick fumbled, and juggled, before finally clinging on. Might it have been different if either the decision or the fumble had turned out otherwise? It matters not. Such is the very essence, the good and bad fortune, of these situations, and Australia had had their share, this summer, of the luck going round. They lost is the long and the short of it and the series went out with a bang and England with a triumph to take some of the edge off earlier disappointment.

Ian and I went down on to the field, as had by now become our custom, to witness the closing ceremony. We were pleased to agree with the choices for man of the match (Tufnell 11 for 93, no contest) and Australia's and England's men of the series (McGrath and Thorpe). On the way out Ian settled his debt with me, the difference between my £5 for the series and his £2.50 on the side bets, less this, finally, than 50p per Test. We then took a bus to Victoria Station where we shook each other by the hand before going our separate ways. It isn't over till it's over, but now it was over. Segmented as may be, interrupted therefore by work and other things, it was one bloody brilliant summer vacation.

Some last observations. I had worried on the eve of the Oval Test about a possible depletion of Australia's bowling resources, but on this wicket they proved more than adequate. It was the batting, rather, that was the problem. It is worth also reminding oneself, perhaps, about the fourth day at Trent Bridge and how it might have been had England battled for the draw then. In all probability it would have been no different, because even survival for a day and a half would have been a tall order. But who knows? As to the series overall, there is much I will treasure from it, including, obviously, the fact that Australia came back from an initial debacle on the first morning to win it. But the thing I will treasure above all is that I had this further opportunity, after 1993, to watch on several days the magnificence that is the bowling of Shane Warne. It is a privilege and a delight to be witness to such excellence, as also to the unique, extrovert, restlessly talkative, sometimes posturing, individuality that is his embodiment of it. As Bradman of McCabe: you will be lucky to see its like again.

An associated displeasure, however, was Warne's reception by a sector of the crowd on all but the two London grounds (to their great credit). At Trent Bridge on the Sunday, there was a moment when an entire, if small, enclosure sang to the rest of the assembly, 'Stand up if you hate Shane Warne', and indeed stood up to sing it. And this went along, at one time and another – at Edgbaston, Old Trafford, Headingley – with the 'You fat bastard' and the 'Ten men, nine men, eight men etc. and their dogs went to bed with Shane Warne'. The intelligence reels. In face of a skill and artistry so phenomenal... that. It may be said here that it is itself a kind of recognition; the same is not sung of, shall we say, Paul Reiffel. But how impoverished and brutalising a sporting culture it is that can offer only this form of recognition to one of the great bowlers of all time. To see it more clearly, just project the thing backwards. Imagine, Bradman at Headingley in 1948: 'You small runt' and the rest. Unimaginable. Debased.

Not to end, though, on the dung-heap. I think also, out of much I have read during and about this series, of two particular pieces by Matthew Engel and Frank Keating: the first – 'Gimme an S gimme a W' – on Shane Warne and Steve Waugh at Old Trafford; the second on Warne – 'the portly sadist' – at Trent Bridge. Two pieces in the best traditions of writing about the game, displaying admiration for a great and worthy foe, admiration if anything enhanced by the slightly rueful note in it. This is the civility of cricket, the doing homage to its majesty above the stakes of battle. In another piece in the latest *Wisden Cricket Monthly*, Engel speaks of Test cricket as 'the greatest form of the greatest game'. How can it be doubted?

Cricket, lovely, matchless Test match cricket. Oh yes, and for next time: 5-0, 17-4; 114-92, 57-37.

II

Thursday

And so to the Oval. Australia's victory at Trent Bridge meant that the big issue was not, after all, to be settled here, but there was still a sense of occasion as the final Test approached. For me the Oval was the setting for my first experience of first-class cricket when, sometime in the 1970s, my mother took me to watch Surrey (her team) play Kent (mine). Knott, Luckhurst and Underwood may well have played for Kent that day, but what stayed with me was not so much the game as the venue. The Oval is simply a very impressive place. Its sheer scale – including that of the playing area – is one aspect of it. The almost majestic pavilion that seems to dwarf all others found in England is a second. The landmark gasholder to one side of the ground is a third, and possibly the best of the lot. My memories of the Oval were by no means all happy. The most recent was of a trip in 1992 to see the fourth day of England versus Pakistan. Then the England tail struggled for a little more than an hour to set Pakistan a total of 2 to win in their second innings. Mark Ramprakash stepped up, bowled a wide for his first delivery and was hit for four by Aamir Sohail off the second. That victory gave Pakistan the series. The most abiding were of TV coverage of 'blackwash' summers in the 1970s when West Indian batsmen dealt all too easily with whatever English bowlers could throw at them. At the Oval in 1976 West Indies made 687 for 8 declared, still one of the highest team totals of all time. Even so, it was good to be back.

To get to the ground on this occasion the first task was to run the gauntlet of ticket touts lined up outside the tube station. I had always thought there was a law against this sort of thing, and that to circumvent it touting was an activity that took place in whispered exchanges down side streets. At the Oval, by contrast, touting took place in loud cockney accents on the main street outside the ground, and police officers simply turned a blind eye. Very south London. The second task was to join a shuffling queue outside the ground and wait 10 minutes before getting in. In this series, this was certainly a first. Thank goodness I had for once arrived with time to spare. The third task was to think up ways of hiding from the sun in what were clearly going to be unshaded seats. Bizarrely, the record books which had been assaulted by rain in June were now threatened by a heatwave in August. Persistent sunshine (and great humidity) since Trent Bridge looked like making this the hottest August in recorded history.

I found Norm taking in the territory at our appointed spot in the Gover Stand at the Vauxhall End. The seats were not bad – third or fourth slippish I suppose – but in row B they were so low down as to give the impression of peering up at proceedings. The downward slope of the ground from pitch to pavilion meant that we couldn't actually see anything of the outfield at the far end of the ground. We figured we would manage provided that the seats in row A in front of us remained empty for the day (which, as it turned out, they did). Having reached this conclusion we chewed the fat for a bit, mainly concentrating on the fact that Atherton had finally won a toss and elected to bat. Good news for England, we thought, especially as the wicket was widely expected to be worth a good few runs: 'the usual true-looking Oval pitch' is how Christopher Martin-Jenkins described it in the *Telegraph*.

We also debated the issue now at the top of the cricketing agenda, Atherton's future as England captain. According to pre-match reports in the papers this matter would be determined chiefly by Atherton himself largely on the basis of what happened in this final Test (which struck Norm and me as odd). The list of potential successors was generally held to comprise Adam Hollioake, Nasser Hussain, Mark Ramprakash and Alec Stewart. The shape of the England team of the near future was also a talking point, sparked in part by the selectors' decision to recall Mark Butcher (in place of John Crawley), Mark Ramprakash (in place of Ben Hollioake), Peter Martin (in place of the injured Dean Headley) and Philip Tufnell (in place of Robert Croft). Although these changes were largely uncontroversial, they revealed the distance England still had to go to come up with a settled team. On the Australian side two team changes had been made, Kasprowicz and Gloucestershire's Tasmanian, Shaun Young, coming in for Gillespie and Reiffel. In this case, however, both changes were enforced, the product of injury (Gillespie) and a problem pregnancy back home (Reiffel). The Australian attack, built around McGrath and Warne, still looked outstanding of course. Norm and I finished by placing our first set of side bets. Ian: Atherton (once again, but I sensed he needed me), Warne, 442. Norm: Stewart, McGrath, 420.

Down to business at 11.00, and a not exactly unprecedented start for England in this series: 24 for 2 in the seventh over, with Butcher bowled McGrath for 5 and Atherton caught Healy bowled McGrath for 8. Atherton at least found a marginally new way to get out, allowing an off-cutter to clip the inside edge of his bat as it made its way into Healy's gloves. The familiar aspect of the dismissal was that it was the seventh time McGrath had claimed Atherton's wicket in the series. It was also McGrath's 150th Test wicket (in his thirty-fourth Test). Thereafter, however, England took the game to the Australians as Stewart and Hussain saw them to 97 for 2 at lunch. Their innings were by no means chanceless, but at least they survived and put together some runs. Even Stevens, we thought, and a pretty good recovery by England.

After the resumption that recovery was quickly wrecked by Australia, again a not unprecedented event. This time the destruction took place in a little less than the full afternoon session, which saw the remaining eight England wickets fall for 83 runs. As in the first innings at Lord's, the chief destroyer was McGrath, who almost on his own reduced the English innings to rubble with figures of 7 for 76 in 21 overs. All the significant wickets were taken by him. Stewart fell lbw to his first ball (in the second over) after lunch. A minor recovery then followed before four further batsmen – Hussain, Thorpe, Hollioake and Ramprakash – were dismissed for four runs as England progressed from 128 for 3 to 132 for 7. Thorpe was bowled by a ball which McGrath slanted across him from round the wicket to take leg stump. Even on the big screen replay it was hard to figure out how this could have happened. Hollioake, the only one of the four not to fall to McGrath, had to endure the embarrassment of leaving a straight one from Shane Warne and watch it remove his middle and off stumps. For once the England tail wagged a bit: 26 not out from Caddick, 20 from Martin, and stands of 26 and 17 for the eighth and ninth wickets (which in the context of all that had gone before were not to be sniffed at). The end was, however, very quick, Malcolm falling lbw to Kasprowicz first ball. Although McGrath's was clearly the outstanding performance of the innings, Kasprowicz had bowled well enough earlier on to deserve a little more than this consolation prize. England 180 all out and an early tea.

Amazingly, Norm had won on all three dimensions of our side bets, Stewart's 36 having been threatened, but to my great disappointment not surpassed, by Hussain's 35 and Thorpe's 27. We agreed that somewhere along the line – Trent Bridge on something like the second day? – we had decided that an extra 50p would be awarded for this feat. In a single innings my hard-won advantage of £3.50 had thus been whittled down to £1.50. All to play for on that front at least. We both thought long and hard before making our choices for the Australian innings. Norm: Mark Waugh (fair enough, for this could certainly be thought to be his wicket), Caddick, 350. Ian: Taylor, Tufnell, 336.

To begin with the Australian innings progressed very nicely. Indeed, in scoring 49 runs off the fast bowlers Elliott and Taylor looked entirely comfortable, with Taylor striking fours at a rapid rate and for once outscoring his opening partner. Then, however, Atherton turned to Tufnell, who opened his return to Test cricket with two wicket maidens to remove both Elliott (bowled for 12) and Taylor (caught Hollioake for 38). Tufnell proceeded to bowl a highly controlled spell of 2 for 6 in 7.1 overs, until rain (which had become increasingly likely in a day that slowly changed from blue skies to grey) intervened to interrupt it. The players went off for 20 minutes from 5.30. Soon after 6.00 they went off again for what turned out to be the last time on the day. Australia 77 for 2 at stumps, with 8.5 overs lost.

Watching all this turned out to be a lot more pleasant than Norm and I had expected: no people in the seats in front, very little sunshine to beam down on our unshaded stand, a bad day for England of course, but that was reasonably predictable. The main chat came from a bunch of advertising executives in the seats behind us, who discussed campaigns for Levi Strauss, Boddington and Coca-Cola, revealed in this context that on the entire planet only the word 'OK' is more widely recognised than 'Coca-Cola', phoned the office to track down Amy and tell some guy to get off another line and speak on this, and generally put the world of advertising to rights. For a period towards the end of the England innings blow-up *Sunday Sport* sheep were bounced around the crowd at the Vauxhall End, but that was pretty much it. Very subdued all round.

Norm and I stayed until play was finally called off at 6.35, then walked to the main exit. 'Atherton on the edge' ran the boards on *Evening Standard* stands. Having stopped for a few minutes to watch some of the Australian players leave the ground (and, in Norm's case, very nearly get Steve Waugh's autograph), we made our way to the Oval tube station. At a bus stop en route who should we see but Geoffrey Boycott asking a woman about the service into town. This seemed to complete a day of odd happenings: wickets falling on a batsman's track, rain bringing an end to a forecast day of sunshine, and now one of the stars of the game queueing to take a bus from the ground. Well, why not?

Friday

The papers did not look fondly on England's first-innings performance. 'Oval and out' ran the headline on the *Guardian*'s sports section. 'Feeble England run up white flag' was the *Times*'s view. The *Independent* cited William Hill's odds on successors to Atherton following the first-day batting collapse: Hussain 10 to 11, Stewart 9 to 4, Hollioake 5 to 2, Russell 20 to 1, Ramprakash 25 to 1. The tabloids were rather more lurid. Norm and I sensed there might be a little more to England's first-innings collapse than met the eye; a less than perfect wicket for instance. In the *Telegraph* Martin-Jenkins hinted at this too, writing of 'a pitch which wasn't quite the blameless beauty of long Oval tradition'. In opening his account of the first day's proceedings he also reported that, for the first time ever, *Test Match Special* was being broadcast on the internet via the Lord's site.

At the beginning of the second day of a Test match expected to be played in sweltering heat, pretty much the first thing we had to contend with was rain. A couple of overs were bowled before one short interruption. Then a couple more. It was a frustrating start, though also a godsend for Norm and me as it sent us in search of cover to the Fender Stand, where we found seats with much more elevation than our abandoned ones in Gover, a vastly superior perspective, and a position in the region of first or second slip. In Fender we were also able to escape Essex man incarnate, sitting directly behind us for this second day in Gover and looking like becoming completely intolerable no more than 20 minutes in. Instead we mingled with City slickers who, between phone calls on their mobiles, complained about the Blair government (interventionist but not prepared to disburse subsidies, so the worst of both worlds), million-pound houses near Notting Hill Gate, and goings-on in the markets. As they also said nothing to move us from their seats, we were happy.

The day's play turned out to be unusual for this series. Although there was little new in 11 wickets going down, only 193 runs were scored and for a day of more than 80 overs that was not at all par for the course. This slow-scoring day turned out, however, to be totally absorbing as Tufnell, bowling unchanged from the Pavilion End, turned in a superb performance to register figures of 7 for 64 in 34.3 overs. He was aggressive, eager, totally in control and a real danger, none of which could be said about Croft except at rare moments in this series. He was also the first England bowler single-handedly to destroy an Australian innings, and the first to return exceptional figures. Only Caddick at Edgbaston (5 for 50) and Gough at Headingley (5 for 149) had even managed five-fors prior to this match. What if? It was inevitable that we would ask this, and also impossible to generate an answer. At the Vauxhall End, Caddick was by far the most effective partner for Tufnell, bowling an excellent line and length and often missing either the bat or off stump by fractions of an inch. He ended with rather unflattering figures of 3 for 76 from 19 overs, including two wickets in two balls towards the end of the Australian innings (a feat he had also managed in the first Test at Edgbaston).

For Australia batsmen came and went, with Blewett top-scoring on 45 despite never looking in touch. He eventually went to an excellent catch by Stewart, who pounced like a cat on a miscue passing down leg-side. Healy's dismissal was the most unusual. Having very nearly been brilliantly stumped by Stewart, he was caught between the keeper's legs later in the same over (and possibly next ball, I forget). Late on there was one key partnership – of 41 between Ponting (40) and Warne (30) – which saw Tufnell hit about a bit and Australia move past England's 180. The question was whether this mattered. At 218 all out, Australia had a first-innings lead of only 38, the smallest of the five England had conceded in Tests since Edgbaston. On the other hand, 38 was equivalent to something like 80 on a 400-run wicket, so maybe it was significant after all. To Norm and me this certainly felt like one of the closest games of the series.

The side bets business between Norm and me was also hotting up. This time I had made the right choices for bowler and innings total. I very nearly got batsman too as Taylor's 38, like Stewart's 36, took on an air of impregnability in a low-scoring innings. It was, however, overhauled by Blewett (almost entirely through squirts off the edge), who went to lunch level with Taylor on 38 before progressing to his 45 thereafter. At the very end of the innings Ponting also made it to 40 before being last out, caught Hussain bowled Tufnell. Fair dos. My lead had moved back up to £2.50. We picked again for the England second innings. Ian: Atherton (too late to switch allegiance now), Warne, 177. Norm: Thorpe, McGrath, 188.

Before long the Australians' lead of 38 began to look very significant indeed. This time Kasprowicz got Atherton, out (again for 8) to a slice picked up routinely enough by Steve Waugh in the gully. There was the odd shout of 'Resign!' as Atherton trudged back to the pavilion, but most people seemed to feel for the guy. It had not been a good series though: 257 runs at 23 and a losing Ashes campaign. Stewart went next, lbw to Kasprowicz. As in the first innings, England were 24 for 2. This time, though, things got worse rather than better. In fading light Warne and (for the first time in the series) Mark Waugh took up the attack. Renewed disbelief from Norm, but Waugh did at least trap Butcher lbw for 13 before being taken for a boundary or two by Thorpe. That was enough for Taylor, who turned to McGrath and, as had no doubt been intended, saw the batsmen accept the umpires' offer of the light. Thorpe's flurry at the finish had taken England from 26 for 3 to 52 for 3 by the close. 14 for 3 in effect.

This was clearly not a healthy position, but Norm and I were not sure precisely how unhealthy it was either. Or, to put it another way, we could not decide what England would need to score to set Australia a testing target. This was, after all, the Oval, and the wicket might therefore be expected still to have some runs in it. On the evidence of the first two days, that might very well not be the case though. Weighing it all up we figured that 200, setting Australia 160-odd to win, was the minimum requirement for England.

Saturday

On the morning of the third day the commentators finally started to come clean about their mistakes of the first two days. This was Mark Nicholas in the *Telegraph*: 'We all got the pitch wrong, wildly wrong: from feather bed to terror track in less than a day'. But there was very little reappraisal of the relative performances of the two teams. If on the first day England had been 'pathetic', 'just humiliating' and so on, had this also been true of the Australians on the second? Or had England actually acquitted themselves reasonably well on a pitch that was dangerous from the start? None of the pundits was prepared to think back that far, and possibly for good reason. There was, after all, the intriguing day ahead to write about.

Passing among the crowd as play started was news that the match statistics had been marginally altered overnight by a decision of the umpires to call a Blewett straight drive off Tufnell six rather than the four given during the second day's play. 47 therefore to Blewett, 7 for 66 for Tufnell, 220 to the Australians and a lead of 40 on first innings. England thus effectively 12 for 3 at the start of the third day instead of 14 for 3. Far more damaging to England's cause than the award of these two runs was, however, the dismissal of Hussain – caught Elliott bowled Warne for 2 – to the third ball of the morning. England effectively 12 for 4. 'It'll be over by lunch' was the resigned judgment of many long-suffering England supporters. 'It's a disgrace! I want back my money!' was the more impassioned view of a West Indian guy sitting several rows behind us. In came Ramprakash to block his first ball from Warne. 'Put your foot down the wicket and hit the ball!' screamed the West Indian.

Ramprakash immediately took the advice. Warne's next delivery was struck cleanly for four, and for a while England prospered as

Thorpe and Ramprakash took the game to the Australians. A lead of 50 was followed by the 50 partnership. As a lead of 100 came within range, however, Thorpe was out to another sensational catch by Taylor at first slip. As at Headingley, Taylor somehow grabbed hold of the ball as it was in the process of speeding past him to make the catch. Incredible. Norm and I felt this must have been something like Taylor's tenth catch of the series, but on checking found it only to be his sixth. His had still been a superb display of slip fielding. England at this point were 131 for 5, effectively 91 for 5. The partnership of 79 between Thorpe and Ramprakash was the biggest of the match to date.

The innings was not wrapped up immediately, as some around us feared it might be, but the curve was clearly downward from here on in. Hollioake was lbw to Kasprowicz for 4 to reduce England to 138 for 6. Ramprakash then hit out before being routinely stumped by Healy off Warne for 48. 160 for 7. When three wickets fell to the first, third and fifth balls of Kasprowicz's sixteenth over – Martin being sharply caught by the bowler, Tufnell being brilliantly taken by Healy, and Malcolm being bowled – it was all over for England. Caddick, in for 50 minutes and 37 balls, was 0 not out at the close of the innings. Kasprowicz, meanwhile, became the third bowler in the match to claim seven wickets in an innings. Indeed, he had the best analysis of the lot: 7 for 36 in 15.5 overs.

England all out for 163 meant that Australia needed 124 in something like two and a half days to win. Even in this match it seemed unlikely to be beyond their powers. But cricket, as I think has been said before, is a funny game, and this match was revealing one of its more peculiar dimensions. It is also, of course, a mind game as much as anything else, and the psychological war was now being waged not merely by the 11 Englishmen in the middle but also by the vast majority of the Oval's full house. Pitted against them were odd couples of Australian batsmen plus Norm, who occasionally responded to English chants with a lonesome 'Come on Aussie!' His was maybe not an entirely solitary voice, but it was certainly a minority one.

The final scene of the final act of the series opened. Both Norm and I (and most of the crowd, no doubt) expected Australia to win. Norm: Elliott, Tufnell, 4 wickets down. Ian: Taylor, Malcolm, 6 wickets down. A single by Taylor off Malcolm's first delivery set the ball rolling. Elliott quickly followed up with a four, only to see

Malcolm claim his wicket lbw. Australia 5 for 1 after four balls had been bowled. The innings had this kind of dramatic structure throughout its 32.1 overs. For Australia the most resistance was put up by the top scorers from the first innings: Taylor (18), Blewett (19) and Ponting (20). A second-wicket partnership of 31 by Taylor and Blewett took the score to 36. A sixth-wicket partnership of 34 by Ponting and Healy took the score to 88. But the Australians could never quite do enough, and the heroes of the hour eventually turned out to be English. Tufnell and Caddick, bowling controlled, inspired spells in tandem for all but seven overs of the Australian innings, did all that could have been asked of them, and more. In support, the entire England team played wonderfully tight cricket and never gave the batsmen an inch. As captain, Atherton was in full control.

'I refuse to be tense about this!' protested Norm, who with the Ashes in the bag had spent most of the match defying the fates, renouncing Jenny's lucky stone and generally trying to look as relaxed as possible. By this stage, however, it was no good. The match was loaded with tension, and no one present could escape it. For a pleasant change it was the Australians who buckled under pressure, rapidly collapsing at the end of their innings as the collective hysteria of the crowd mounted and the batsmen became more and more hemmed in. Five wickets fell for 16 runs to reduce Australia to 104 all out and give England victory by 19 runs. England of course had some luck in securing their victory: that Warne was limping and needed a runner; that a caught and bowled chance offered by Healy was initially fumbled but eventually claimed by Caddick. But, dammit, they deserved it.

At the close – around 5.25 – Norm and I joined the crowd in front of the pavilion to see Atherton collect a cheque for the match and Taylor a replica urn for the series. Tufnell, the only player in the series to take 10 wickets in a match, was named man of this match by Tony Lewis. McGrath and Thorpe were named men of the series by the two team coaches. It was hard to disagree with these verdicts, though I guess Healy could just as easily have been selected as top Aussie. Australia, having been dismissed for 118 in 31.5 overs and 150 minutes at the start of the series, had been dismissed for 104 in 32.1 overs and 153 minutes at the finish. England had thereby won the first and last Tests. In between, of course, Australia had won the Ashes. Shame that. I had, however, come out £2.50 up in side bets with Norm, though I had lost a fiver to him on the series result.

The end of the line then. 3-2 to Australia was certainly not how I had wanted things to turn out, but it was impossible to argue with the result. Indeed, 3-2 was flattering to England: either 3-1 or 4-2 would have been a fairer reflection on the cricket played by the two teams in the series. Thinking back over all that had happened, Australian performances stood out most: Taylor's century at Edgbaston, Elliott's at Lord's, Steve Waugh's two hundreds at Old Trafford and the Healy stumping there, Ponting's hundred at Headingley, the bowling of McGrath and Warne pretty much throughout, and some superb catches behind the wicket by Healy, Taylor and Mark Waugh. This was a formidable Australian team and I was sad to see them go. Indeed, watching great cricketers like Mark Taylor and Ian Healy leave an English Test arena for what had to be the final time was almost like saying goodbye to old friends. Walking away from this series once the presentations were over was certainly also an act of bidding farewell to a central part of my life in the summer of 1997. In 1745.4 overs, 5610 runs had been scored (at 3.2 per over) and 198 wickets taken. Norm and I had scarcely missed a ball – maybe 10 or 12 each, though not the same 10 or 12 in our two cases – and we had certainly not missed a single wicket or significant scoring stroke. It scarcely seemed possible that this whole unfolding drama had been packed into the equivalent of less than 20 full days of Test cricket.

As for the future, Australia at the end of this Ashes series looked well set whether or not Taylor chose to call it a day after 33 Tests as captain. The new generation – Blewett, Elliott, Gillespie, McGrath and Ponting – was already well established and likely to form the nucleus of Australian teams for some time to come. On the English side, the Michael Atherton question had of course been given a new twist by the manner of the series' finish, and opinion was now divided over whether he should step down after 46 Tests in charge. 'Mike him stay' argued the *News of the World*, which seemed a bit rich after the criticism meted out just weeks earlier. But whoever captains England in the late 1990s will have his work cut out to generate performances capable of troubling top international teams more than sporadically.

In 1997 the Australians, best team of the lot, were worthy winners of a fine series. I salute them.

Series averages

England batting and fielding

	M	I	NO	Runs	HS	Ave	100	50	Ct/St
G P Thorpe	6	11	2	453	138	50.33	1	3	8/-
N Hussain	6	11	0	431	207	39.18	2	0	8/-
M A Ealham	4	6	3	105	53*	35.00	0	1	3/-
J P Crawley	5	9	1	243	83	30.37	0	2	3/-
M R Ramprakash	1	2	0	52	48	26.00	0	0	0/-
M A Butcher	5	10	0	254	87	25.40	0	2	8/-
A J Stewart	6	12	1	268	87	24.36	0	1	23/-
M A Atherton	6	12	1	257	77	23.36	0	2	2/-
B C Hollioake	1	2	0	30	28	15.00	0	0	1/-
A J Hollioake	2	4	0	51	45	12.75	0	0	4/-
P J Martin	1	2	0	23	20	11.50	0	0	1/-
A R Caddick	5	8	2	59	26*	9.83	0	0	1/-
D W Headley	3	6	2	39	22	9.75	0	0	1/-
R D B Croft	5	8	0	75	24	9.37	0	0	1/-
A M Smith	1	2	1	4	4*	4.00	0	0	0/-
D E Malcolm	4	5	1	12	12	3.00	0	0	2/-
D Gough	4	6	0	17	10	2.83	0	0	0/-
P C R Tufnell	1	2	0	1	1	0.50	0	0	0/-

England bowling

	Overs	M	Runs	W	Ave	5/10	Best
P C R Tufnell	47.4	22	93	11	8.45	1/1	7-66
M A Ealham	58.4	11	191	8	23.87	0/0	3-60
A R Caddick	179.5	27	634	24	26.41	2/0	5-42
A J Hollioake	19	2	55	2	27.50	0/0	2-31
D W Headley	131.2	20	444	16	27.75	0/0	4-72
D Gough	142	27	511	16	31.93	1/0	5-149
B C Hollioake	15	2	83	2	41.50	0/0	1-26
D E Malcolm	93	19	307	6	51.16	0/0	3-100
R D B Croft	161.5	41	439	8	54.87	0/0	3-125
M A Butcher	2	0	14	0	–	0/0	–
P J Martin	9	5	51	0	–	0/0	–
A M Smith	23	2	89	0	–	0/0	–

Australia batting and fielding

	M	I	NO	Runs	HS	Ave	100	50	Ct/St
P R Reiffel	4	6	3	179	54*	59.66	0	1	1/-
M T G Elliott	6	10	0	556	199	55.60	2	2	4/-
R T Ponting	3	5	0	241	127	48.20	1	0	1/-
S R Waugh	6	10	0	390	116	39.00	2	1	4/-
G S Blewett	6	10	0	381	125	38.10	1	2	9/-
M A Taylor	6	10	0	317	129	31.70	1	1	6/-
I A Healy	6	10	1	225	63	25.00	0	1	25/2
M E Waugh	6	10	0	209	68	20.90	0	2	6/-
S K Warne	6	10	0	188	53	18.80	0	1	2/-
G D McGrath	6	8	6	25	20*	12.50	0	0	2/-
J N Gillespie	4	7	2	57	28*	11.40	0	0	3/-
M G Bevan	3	5	0	43	24	8.60	0	0	1/-
M S Kasprowicz	3	4	0	21	17	5.25	0	0	2/-
S Young	1	2	1	4	4*	4.00	0	0	0/-

Australia bowling

	Overs	M	Runs	W	Ave	5/10	Best
M E Waugh	7	3	16	1	16.00	0/0	1-16
G D McGrath	249.5	67	701	36	19.47	2/0	8-38
J N Gillespie	91.4	20	332	16	20.75	1/0	7-37
M S Kasprowicz	93.3	19	310	14	22.14	1/0	7-36
S K Warne	237.1	69	577	24	24.04	1/0	6-48
P R Reiffel	112.1	28	293	11	26.63	1/0	5-49
M G Bevan	34.4	6	121	2	60.50	0/0	1-14
G S Blewett	3	0	17	0	–	0/0	–
S R Waugh	20	3	76	0	–	0/0	–
S Young	8	3	13	0	–	0/0	–